H.C Beeching

Lyra Sacra, a book of religious verse selected and arranged by H. C. Beeching

H.C Beeching

Lyra Sacra, a book of religious verse selected and arranged by H. C. Beeching

ISBN/EAN: 9783743322356

Manufactured in Europe, USA, Canada, Australia, Japa

Cover: Foto ©Lupo / pixelio.de

Manufactured and distributed by brebook publishing software
(www.brebook.com)

H.C Beeching

Lyra Sacra, a book of religious verse selected and arranged by H. C. Beeching

LYRA SACRA

A BOOK OF RELIGIOUS VERSE

SELECTED AND ARRANGED BY

H. C. BEECHING, M.A.

METHUEN & CO.
36 ESSEX STREET, W.C.
LONDON
1895

PREFACE

THE English are, or at any rate were, a very serious people, and therefore to bring a representative collection of their religious poetry within the compass of a single handy volume requires an editor to draw his lines of limitation sharply and clearly. The principles that have governed the present anthology are these: first, that while being representative on the whole of the current of religious verse, it should not necessarily represent any particular period that fell short in certain essential characteristics. Accordingly, the eighteenth century, which, however interesting in many respects, was not especially poetical or religious, supplies but twenty pages as against the hundred and fifty from the seventeenth. A second canon of choice has been, that no piece, however theologically sound or devotionally fervid, should find place which had not about it a genuine ring of poetry; and, by complement, that none should be admitted which was poetical in treatment but not distinctly religious in temper, or which dealt with religious subjects picturesquely rather than devotionally;—a rule that excluded, for example, such fine pieces as Milton's "Nativity Ode," Southwell's "Burning Babe," and many other poems and carols relating to Christmas and Epiphany.[1] In the third place, the book has not been burdened with hymns to be found in every collection; so that religious poets, whose writing has chiefly taken this form, such as Cowper and Wesley, and in more modern days Lyte and Bonar, may seem rather unkindly treated. Lastly, the Editor determined that paraphrases of the Psalms, an exercise attempted by most of the seventeenth-century poets, and by some very happily, should be reserved for an independent collection.

The standard of excellence has been kept as high as possible, but the very circumstances of the case prevent its being uniform. The high-water mark of the religious lyric in England is fixed by Herbert; Vaughan in one or two pieces reaches as high; so in another style do Crashaw and Marvell: but an anthology restricted to the best work of these few poets, and the one or two of our own day who might rank with them, would lack variety, which is its chief essential. An anthology must,

---

[1] These have been by way of atonement collected by the Editor into a "Book of Christmas Verse," which Mr. Walter Crane has illustrated (Methuens).

by its nature, admit excellence in many degrees and in many styles. In pursuit of this various excellence the Editor has cast his net as wide as possible. He has opened the book with the anonymous poets of the fifteenth century, now first restored from their honourable limbo in the reprints of learned societies to the full light and warmth of English homes. The occasional strangeness of the vocabulary or stiffness of the metre should not hinder the appreciation of so lovely an allegory as *Quia Amore Langueo*, or such direct and simple appeals as " Be my comfort, Christ Jesu," and "Jesu, Lord, that madest me." In the sixteenth and seventeenth centuries it has not been the Editor's good fortune to add any new stars to the map of the heavens, but he may claim that certain of the brighter luminaries, Donne, Giles Fletcher, and Crashaw, are here for the first time exhibited to the public in their proper greatness. In regard to Herbert, the question of choice has been a difficult one. On the one hand, it seemed absurd to transfer to an anthology some forty or fifty pages of a volume which is on the shelves, if not in the memory, of every educated Christian; on the other, it seemed equally absurd to pass him by. Accordingly, twenty pages have been allotted to him *honoris causa*; and these have been filled with what in the Editor's judgment are his best poems, or their finest passages. To give more point to the selection, the pieces here given have been somewhat elaborately annotated. Herbert has suffered much, if not in esteem, yet in usefulness, from the laziness or incapacity of his editors, who pretend to think him an author who requires no elucidation. Even Dr. Grosart, to whom lovers of poetry owe an incalculable debt, while he devotes much space to the "Church Porch," has very few notes on the poems, and those chiefly glossarial. A competent edition of Herbert is much to be desired. In regard to Herbert's disciple, Henry Vaughan, there is less difficulty of choice, because, though as voluminous as Herbert, his work is not nearly so well known, and is much more unequal. Some dozen pieces represent his effective contribution to sacred poetry.[1]

The difficulty recurs this century in the case of Keble. The *Christian Year* had reached its 145th edition before the copyright expired in 1872, so that still fewer readers of religious poetry require to be introduced to it than to the "Temple." Ten pages seemed an ample acknowledgment of its author's worth, and a fair proportionate representation; and these

---

[1] I may be allowed here to refer to an essay of mine contributed to an edition of Vaughan, shortly to be published by Messrs. Laurence & Bullen in their "Muses' Library," in which is examined the much-debated question of Vaughan's debt to Herbert.

the Editor has filled less with whole poems than with selected stanzas which rise above the level of their surroundings. Of the names that mark the course of religious poetry since Keble, many will be familiar to the general reader. He will expect some recognition of the refined feeling and scholarship of Archbishop Trench, the fervour of Dr. Faber, the severe grace of Dr. Newman; perhaps also, in a different school, of Clough and Arnold and Kingsley; and, thanks to the kindness of the holders of copyright, he will not be disappointed. Whether he will expect the inclusion of the still greater names of Tennyson and Browning, will probably depend upon his knowledge of their market value. As the Editor is not allowed to quote from the one, and cannot afford to quote from the other, he must be content with calling attention to an early poem of Lord Tennyson's, called "On a Mourner," which has probably escaped the notice of many readers, as it was slipped in before "You ask me why, tho' ill at ease," in a late edition; and with professing how much the religious thought of our day has gained from the sparks struck out by the genius of Mr. Browning. From living poets the Editor has received uniform kindness, and the reader will understand that for the presence of their poems in these pages he has in every case to thank the author. These new wares he will probably take more delight in scrutinising for himself than in having them cried by the Editor; who will therefore but assure him in conclusion that he will find at least three poets whose works have not before been represented in an anthology, and two others, poems by whom are here for the first time printed.

Yattenden Rectory,
January 1895.

CONTENTS

	PAGE
ANONYMOUS	
BE MY COMFORT, CHRIST JESUS!	1
PRAYER OF RICHARD DE CASTRE	4
QUIA AMORE LANGUEO	6
GEOFFREY CHAUCER	
VIRGINIBUS PUERISQUE	11
SIR WALTER RALEGH	
PILGRIMAGE	12
WRITTEN IN HIS BIBLE THE NIGHT BEFORE HIS EXECUTION	12
EDMUND SPENSER	
THE MINISTRY OF ANGELS	14
EASTER DAY	15
THE LOVE OF CHRIST	15
SIR PHILIP SIDNEY	
SONNET	19
FULKE GREVILLE, LORD BROOKE	
FAITH AND WORKS	20
ROBERT SOUTHWELL	
MAN'S CIVIL WAR	21
AT HOME IN HEAVEN	22
LOST GRACE	23
SAMUEL DANIEL	
FAITH AND FORM	24
WORKS	24

SIR JOHN DAVIES

	PAGE
SELF-KNOWLEDGE	26
SELF-IGNORANCE	27

SIR HENRY WOTTON

THE CHARACTER OF A HAPPY LIFE	28
HYMN	29
A HYMN TO MY GOD	31

DEAN JOHN DOUNE

FOUR SONNETS:

I. *Thou hast made me, and shall Thy work decay?*	32
II. *As due by many titles, I resign*	32
III. *At the round earth's imagin'd corners blow*	33
IV. *Death, be not proud, though some have called thee*	34
LITANY	35
A HYMN TO GOD THE FATHER	36
HYMN TO GOD IN MY SICKNESS	37
GOOD FRIDAY—*RIDING WESTWARD*	37
EASTER DAY	39
THE CROSS	39
CHRIST THE JUDGE	40
CROSSES	40

BEN JONSON

AN HYMN TO GOD THE FATHER	41
TO HEAVEN	42
THE FORTRESS OF MANSOUL	43

WILLIAM DRUMMOND

A HYMN OF THE RESURRECTION	45
FAITH WITHOUT WORKS	45
CHANGE SHOULD BREED CHANGE	46

ROBERT HERRICK

LITANY	47
ETERNITY	48
TO HIS CONSCIENCE	49
LENT	50
TO DEATH	51
TO FIND GOD	51
UPON GOD	52
HUMILITY	52

CONTENTS

GILES FLETCHER
THE INCARNATION	53
THE PASSION	55
THE RESURRECTION	58
EARTH AND HEAVEN	59

GEORGE HERBERT
FROM "THE CHURCH PORCH"
Education	61
Wealth	62
Friendship	62
Conduct	63
Health	64
MATTENS	64
PRAISE	65
SIN	66
THE PEARL	67
THE PULLEY	69
MAN'S MEDLEY	70
THE QUIP	71
THE COLLAR	72
THE PILGRIMAGE	74
DISCIPLINE	75
THE FLOWER	77
THE ELIXIR	79
EMPLOYMENT	80
DIALOGUE	81
CHURCH MUSIC	81
PRAISE	82
THE BIRD	83
THE TEMPER	84
REGENERATION	84
DIVINITY	84

FRANCIS QUARLES
FALSE WORLD	85
THE THRESHING FLOOR	87
THE FOIL	89
THE LOADSTONE	90
THE BIRDCAGE	93

THOMAS CAMPION
THE CHRISTIAN STOIC	94
SONG	95
SONG	96

A. W.
DIALOGUE	97
THOUGH LATE, MY HEART, YET TURN AT LAST	98

WILLIAM SHAKESPEARE
    SOUL AND BODY 100

F. B. P.
    URBS BEATA HIERUSALEM . . . 101

ANONYMOUS
    THE INVITATION 105
    THE HEART'S CHAMBERS . . . 106
    CONFESSION 107
    A ROYAL GUEST 107

R. CRASHAW
    A SONG OF DIVINE LOVE . . . 109
    EASTER DAY 109
    CHRIST WHEN HE DIED 110
    TO THE NAME ABOVE EVERY NAME, THE NAME OF JESUS: *A HYMN* 111
    THE DEAR BARGAIN 116
    S. MARY MAGDALENE 118
    A HYMN TO S. TERESA 119
    UPON THE BOOK AND PICTURE OF THE SERAPHICAL SAINT TERESA . . . 124

SIR W. DAVENANT
    LIFE AND DEATH 125

W. HABINGTON
    NOX NOCTI INDICAT SCIENTIAM . . 126

SIR THOMAS BROWNE
    AN EVENING PRAYER 128

JOHN MILTON
    MORNING HYMN 129
    THE SPACIOUS FIRMAMENT . . . 131
    UPON THE CIRCUMCISION . . . 132
    GOD'S PROVIDENCE 133
    ON HIS BLINDNESS 135
    AT A SOLEMN MUSIC 136
    ON TIME—*TO BE SET ON A CLOCK-CASE* . 137

BISHOP JEREMY TAYLOR
    HYMN FOR ADVENT 139
    A PRAYER FOR CHARITY . . . 140

CONTENTS

ALEXANDER ROSSE
    AFFLICTION 141

JOHN MASON
    A GENERAL SONG OF PRAISE TO ALMIGHTY
        GOD 142
    "THERE REMAINETH A REST". . . 144
    THE PEACE OF GOD 145

JOSEPH BEAUMONT
    THE HOUSE OF THE MIND . . . 147

HENRY MORE
    RESOLUTION 148
    THE PHILOSOPHER'S DEVOTION . . . 150

RICHARD BAXTER
    THE EXIT 153

ANDREW MARVELL
    A DIALOGUE BETWEEN THE RESOLVED SOUL
        AND CREATED PLEASURE . . . 156
    ON A DROP OF DEW 159

HENRY VAUGHAN
    MATTINS 162
    MAN 162
    THE RETREAT 164
    ETENIM RES CREATÆ EXERTO CAPITE OB-
        SERVANTES EXPECTANT REVELATIONEM
        FILIORUM DEI 165
    DESERT 166
    LOVE AND DISCIPLINE 167
    LIBERTY 168
    THE WORLD 169
    PROVIDENCE 170
    THE RAINBOW 171
    THE NIGHT 172
    DEPARTED FRIENDS 174
    THE DAWNING 176

JOHN BUNYAN
    THE SHEPHERD BOY'S SONG IN THE VALLEY
        OF HUMILIATION 178

JOHN NORRIS
    THE ASPIRATION 179

ANONYMOUS
	PAGE
FOR CHRISTMAS	180
LITANY	181
THE WAYS OF WISDOM	182
THE CHILD'S DEATH	184

JOSEPH ADDISON
AN ODE 185

DR. ISAAC WATTS
A SIGHT OF HEAVEN IN SICKNESS . . 186

JOHN BYROM
THE DESPONDING SOUL'S WISH . . 188
THE ANSWER 188
THE SOUL'S TENDENCY TOWARDS ITS TRUE CENTRE 189
DIVINE EPIGRAMS:
  I. *No faith towards God can e'er subsist with wrath* . . . 190
  II. *Think, and be careful what thou art within* 190
  III. *Let thy repentance be without delay* . 190
  IV. *Hath not the potter power to make his clay* 190

CHARLES WESLEY
WRESTLING WITH THE ANGEL . . . 191

WILLIAM COWPER
LIGHT OUT OF DARKNESS . . . 194
THE CONTRITE HEART 195

THOMAS CHATTERTON
FAITH 196

GEORGE CRABBE
THE PILGRIM 198

WILLIAM BLAKE
THE NEW JERUSALEM:
  I. *England, awake! awake! awake!* . 199
  II. *And did those feet in ancient time* . 199
THE TWO SONGS 200
AUGURIES OF INNOCENCE . . . 201
DIVINE EPIGRAMS:
  I. *A tear is an intellectual thing* . 202
  II. *I was angry with my friend* . . 202
  III. *Mutual forgiveness of each vice* . 202
  IV. *The door of death is made of gold* . 202

CONTENTS xvii

WILLIAM WORDSWORTH

PAGE
ODE TO DUTY 203
THE INFLUENCE OF NATURE . . . 205
AN EVENING VOLUNTARY . . . 206
WRITTEN IN KING'S COLLEGE CHAPEL, CAM-
BRIDGE 209
TRUTH AND CHANGE 209
CHILDHOOD AND AGE 210

SAMUEL TAYLOR COLERIDGE

THE NATIVITY 213
TO HIS CHILD 214
ON HIS BAPTISMAL BIRTHDAY . . . 215
JOY 216

HARTLEY COLERIDGE

THE JUST SHALL LIVE BY FAITH . . 218
PRAYER:
   I. *There is an awful quiet in the air* . 218
   II. *Be not afraid to pray—to pray is right* . 219

JOHN KEBLE

HOLY BAPTISM 220
ANGELS AND CHILDREN 221
THE TWO COVENANTS 222
THE WATERFALL 223
SONG OF THE MANNA-GATHERERS . . 224
THE VOICE OF NATURE 225
PREVENIENT GRACE 226
LONELINESS 227
SOWING AND REAPING 227
THE POWER OF PRAYER . . . 228
PENANCE 228
THE BURIAL OF THE DEAD . . . 229

FELICIA DOROTHEA HEMANS

DE PROFUNDIS 231

CARDINAL NEWMAN

SEPARATION OF FRIENDS . . . 232
A VOICE FROM AFAR 233
WAITING FOR THE MORNING . . . 234

JOHN STERLING

WHEN UP TO NIGHTLY SKIES WE GAZE . 236

ARCHBISHOP TRENCH

	PAGE
THE KINGDOM OF GOD	237
NOT THOU FROM US, O LORD, BUT WE	238
LORD, MANY TIMES I AM AWEARY QUITE	239
A GENIAL MOMENT OFT HAS GIVEN	239
LINES WRITTEN AFTER HEARING SOME BEAUTIFUL SINGING IN A CONVENT CHURCH AT ROME	240
THE HOLY EUCHARIST	242
PRAYER	243
COUPLETS	245

ELIZABETH BARRETT BROWNING

HEAVEN AND EARTH	247
WORK	247
BEREAVEMENT	248
SUBSTITUTION	249
THE PROSPECT	249

FREDERICK WILLIAM FABER

SUNDAY	251
LOW SPIRITS	253
THE AGONY	254
THE SORROWFUL WORLD	256

THOMAS TOKE LYNCH

HALLELUJAH!	261
STARS	263
PRAYER	264
INCONSTANCY	266

CHARLES KINGSLEY

A NUN'S SONG	267
A MOTHER'S SONG	268

ARTHUR HUGH CLOUGH

"OLD THINGS NEED NOT BE THEREFORE TRUE"	269
SAY NOT, THE STRUGGLE NOUGHT AVAILETH	269
WHERE LIES THE LAND TO WHICH THE SHIP WOULD GO?	270

MATTHEW ARNOLD

DESIRE	271
MORALITY	273

CONTENTS

THOMAS BLACKBURNE
PAGE
- AN EASTER HYMN 275

COVENTRY PATMORE
- MAGNA EST VERITAS 277
- REMEMBERED GRACE 277
- VICTORY IN DEFEAT 279
- THE TOYS 281
- "LET BE!" 283

GEORGE MACDONALD
- LONGING 285

DORA GREENWELL
- IN SPRING THE GREEN LEAVES SHOOT . 287
- THE LESSON 287
- ONE FRIEND 288
- THE THYME 289
- DECLENSION AND REVIVAL . . . 290
- A THOUGHT AT MIDNIGHT . . . 292
- FAINT YET PURSUING—*A SONG OF THE CHURCH MILITANT* 292
- VENI, VENI EMMANUEL 293

CHRISTINA ROSSETTI
- A NEW AND OLD YEAR SONG . . . 295
- A BRUISED REED 296
- FROM HOUSE TO HOME . . . 297
- "THE WILL OF THE LORD BE DONE" . 299
- "THAT WHERE I AM, THERE YE MAY BE ALSO" 299
- SOONER OR LATER: YET AT LAST . . 300
- A CHILL BLANK WORLD. YET OVER THE UTMOST SEA 302
- O FOOLISH SOUL! TO MAKE THY COUNT . 303
- "A VAIN SHADOW" 303

FREDERICK MYERS
- S. PAUL *speaks* 304

EDWARD DOWDEN
- AH, THAT SHARP THRILL THROUGH ALL MY FRAME! 311
- A SPEAKER TO GOD 312

CONTENTS

GERARD HOPKINS
	PAGE
BARNFLOOR AND WINEPRESS	313
GOD'S GRANDEUR	314
HEAVEN HAVEN	315
MORNING, MIDDAY, AND EVENING SACRIFICE	316

ROBERT BRIDGES
JOY	317
SINCE TO BE LOVED ENDURES	319
THIS WORLD IS UNTO GOD A WORK OF ART	320
WHEN I SEE CHILDHOOD ON THE THRESHOLD SEIZE	320
THESE MEAGRE RHYMES WHICH A RETURNING MOOD	321
PATER NOSTER	322
LAUS DEO	322

DIGBY MACKWORTH DOLBEN
THE SHRINE	323
"OSCULO ORIS SUI OSCULETUR ME"	324
REQUESTS	326

ROBERT LOUIS STEVENSON
THE CELESTIAL SURGEON	327
THE HOUSE BEAUTIFUL	328

FRANCIS THOMPSON
THE HOUND OF HEAVEN	330

NOTES 337

INDEX 357

LYRA SACRA

BE MY COMFORT, CHRIST JESUS!

Jesus that sprang of Jesse's root,
As us hath preached the prophete,
Flower and fruit both soft and soote [1]
To mannis soul of savour sweet;
Jesu, Thou broughtest man to boot
When Gabriel gan Mary greet,
To fell our foemen under foot,
In her Thou sit'st a seemly seat;
A maiden was Thy mother meet,
Of whom Thou tookest flesh for us;
As ye may both my balës beet,[2]
So be my comfort, Christ Jesus.

Jesu, Thou art wisdom of wit,
Of Thy Father full of might!
Mannis soul to saven it,
In poor apparel Thou wert dight.
Jesu, Thou were in cradle knit

[1] Sweet.   [2] Amend.

In weedë wrapped both day and night,
In Bethlehem born, as the gospel writ,
With angels' song and heaven light.
Bairn y-born of a birdë [1] bright,
Full courteous was Thy comely cus ; [2]
Through virtue of that sweetë light,
So be my comfort, Christ Jesus.

Jesu, that were of yearës young,
Fair and fresh of hide and hue,
When Thou were in thraldom throng [3]
And tormented with many a Jew ;
When blood and water were out-wrong,
For beating was Thy body blue ;
As a clod of clay Thou were for-clong, [4]
So dead in trough [5] then men Thee threw.
But grace out of Thy gravë grew ;
Thou rose up quick, comfort to us.
For her love that this counsel knew,
So be my comfort, Christ Jesus.

Jesu, soothfast God and Man,
Two kindis knit in one persone,
The wonder work that Thou began,
Thou hast fulfilled in flesh and bone.
Out of this world wytely [6] Thou wan,
Lifting up Thyself alone ;
For mightily Thou rose, and ran
Straight unto Thy Father in throne.

[1] Maid. [2] Kiss. [3] Driven.
[4] Shrunk. [5] Grave. [6] Actively.

Now dare man make no morë moan;
For man it is Thou wroughtë thus,
And God with man is made at one,
So be my comfort, Christ Jesus.

Jesu, my sovereign Saviour,
Almighty God, there be no mo;
Christ, be Thou my Governour,
Thy faith let me not fallen fro.
Jesu, my joy and my succour,
In my body and soul also,
God, be Thou my strongest food,
And wis[1] Thou me when me is woe.
Lord, Thou makest friend of foe,
Let me not live in languor thus,
But see my sorrow, and say now "ho!"[2]
And be my comfort, Christ Jesus.

Jesu, to Thee I cry and greed,[3]
Prince of Peace, to Thee I pray;
Thou wouldest bleed for mannis need,
And suffer many a fearful fray.
Thou me feed in all my dread
With patïencë now and ay
My life to lead in word and deed,
As is most pleasant to Thy pay,[4]
And to die well when it is my day.
Jesu, that died on tree for us,
Let me not be the fiendis prey,
But be my comfort, Christ Jesus.   Amen.

[1] Guide.   [2] *i.e.* Stay it.   [3] Moan.   [4] Pleasure.

PRAYER OF RICHARD DE CASTRE

Jesu, Lord, that madest me,
   And with Thy blessed blood hast bought,
Forgive that I have grieved Thee
   With word, with will, and eke with thought.

Jesu, in whom is all my trust,
   That died upon the roodë tree,
Withdraw my heart from fleshly lust
   And from all worldly vanity.

Jesu, for thy woundës smart
   On feet and on Thy handës two,
Make me meek and low of heart,
   And Thee to love as I should do.

Jesu, for Thy bitter wound
   That wentë to Thine heartë root,
For sin that hath my heartë bound
   Thy blessed blood must be my boot.

And Jesu Christ, to Thee I call,
   That art God, full of might,
Keep me clean, that I ne fall
   In deadly sin by day ne night.

Jesu, grant me mine asking,
   Perfect patience in my disease;
And never might I do that thing
   Should Thee in any wise displease.

Jesu, that art our heavenly King,
   Soothfast God and Man also,
Give me grace of good ending
   And them that I am holden to.

Jesu, for the deadly tears
   That Thou sheddest for my guilt,
Hear and speed Thou my prayers
   And spare me that I be not spilt.

Jesu, for them I Thee beseech
   That wrathen Thee in any wise,
Withhold from them Thy hand of wreach [1]
   And let them live in Thy service.

Jesu, most comfort for to see
   Of Thy saintis evereachone,[2]
Comfort them that careful be,
   And help them that be woe-begone.

Jesu, keep them that be good,
   Amend them that have grieved Thee,
And send them fruits of earthly food
   As each man need'th in his degree.

Jesu, that art withouten lees [3]
   Almighty God in Trinity,
Cease these wars, and send us peace
   With lasting love and charity.

[1] Vengeance.   [2] Everyone.   [3] Lies.

Jesu, that art the ghostly stone
  Of Holy Church in middle earth,
Bring Thy folds and flocks in one
  And rule them rightly with one herd.

Jesu, for Thy blessedful blood
  Bring, if Thou wilt, the souls to bliss
From whom I have had any good,
  And spare that they have done amiss. Amen.

QUIA AMORE LANGUEO

In a valley of this restless mind
I sought in mountain and in mead,
Trusting a true love for to find.
Upon an hill then took I heed ;
A voice I heard (and near I yede [1])
In great dolour complaining tho : [2]
See, dear soul, how my sides bleed :
Quia amore langueo.

Upon this hill I found a tree,
Under the tree a man sitting ;
From head to foot wounded was he,
His heartë blood I saw bleeding.
A seemly man to be a king,
A gracious face to look unto.
I asked why he had paining :
He said, *Quia amore langueo.*

[1] Went.   [2] Then.

I am true love that false was never;
My sister, man's soul, I loved her thus.
Because we would in no wise dissever,
I left my kingdom glorious.
I purveyed her a palace full precious;
She fled, I followed, I loved her so,
That I suffered this pain piteous,
Quia amore langueo.

My fair love and my spousë bright!
I saved her fro beating, and she hath me bet;
I clothed her in grace and heavenly light,
This bloody shirt she hath on me set:
For longing of love yet would I not let;
Sweetë strokës are these: lo!
I have loved her ever as I her het,[1]
Quia amore langueo.

I crowned her with bliss, and she me with thorn;
I led her to chamber, and she me to die;
I brought her to worship, and she me to scorn,
I did her reverence, and she me villainy.
To love that loveth is no maistry:[2]
Her hate made never my love her foe—
Ask me then no question why—
Quia amore langueo.

Look unto mine handes, man!
These gloves were given me when I her sought;

[1] Promised.   [2] Need.

They be not white, but red and wan;
Embroidered with blood my spouse them brought;
They will not off, I loose them nought,
I woo her with them wherever she go.
These hands for her so friendly fought,
Quia amore langueo.

Marvel not, man, though I sit still:
See, love hath shod me wonder strait,
Buckled my feet, as was her will,
With sharpë nails (well thou mayest wait!).
In my love was never desait,
All my members I have opened her to;
My body I made her heartes bait,[1]
Quia amore langueo.

In my side I have made her nest;
Look in; how wide a wound is here!
This is her chamber, here shall she rest,
That she and I may sleep in fere.[2]
Here may she wash if any filth were,
Here is succour for all her woe;
Come when she will she shall have cheer,
Quia amore langueo.

I will abide till she be ready;
I will her sue or she say nay;
If she be retchless I will be greedy,
If she be dangerous I will her pray;

---

[1] Resting-place. [2] Together.

If she do weep, then bide I ne may:
Mine arms been spread to clip her me to.
Cry once, I come: now soul, assay
Quia amore langueo.

Fairë love, let us go play,
Apples been ripe in my gardine;
I shall thee clothe in a new array,
Thy meat shall be milk, honey and wine.
Fairë love, let us go dine;
Thy sustenance is in my scrip, lo!
Tarry not now, my fair spouse mine,
Quia amore langueo.

If thou be foul, I shall thee make clean,
If thou be sick, I shall thee heal;
If thou mourn aught, I shall thee mene.[1]
Spouse, why wilt thou not with me deal?
Foundest thou ever love so leal?
What wilt thou, soul, that I shall do?
I may not unkindly thee appeal,
Quia amore langueo.

What shall I do now with my spouse
But abide her of my gentleness,
Till that she look out of her house
Of fleshly affection? love mine she is;
Her bed is made, her bolster is bliss,
Her chamber is chosen; is there none mo.
Look out at the window of kindëness,
Quia amore langueo.

[1] Care for.

My love's in her chamber, hold your peace!
Make no noise, but let her sleep;
My babe shall suffer no disease,
I may not hear my dear child weep.
With my pap I shall her keep,
Ne marvel ye not though I tend her to;
This hole in my side had ne'er been so deep,
But *quia amore langueo.*

Long and love thou never so high,
My love is more than thine may be;
Thou gladdest, thou weepest, I sit thee by;
Yet wouldst thou once, love, look at me!
Should I alway feedë thee
With children's meat? nay, love, not so!
I will prove thy love with adversity,
Quia amore langueo.

Wax not weary, mine ownë wife!
What meed is aye to live in comfórt?
In tribulation I reign more rife
Ofter timës than in disport.
In weal and in woe I am aye to support,
Mine ownë wife, go not me fro!
Thy meed is marked, when thou are mort,
Quia amore langueo.

Anon.

VIRGINIBUS PUERISQUE

O youngë freshë folkës, he or she,
   In which that love upgroweth with your age,
Repaireth home from worldly vanity,
   And of your heart upcasteth the visage
   To thilkë God, that after His image
   You made, and thinketh all nis [1] but a fair,
This world that passeth soon, as flowrës fair.

And loveth Him the which that, right for love,
   Upon a cross, our soulës for to buy,
First starf [2] and rose, and sits in heaven above;
   For He nil [1] falsen no wight, dare I say,
   That will His heart all wholly on Him lay;
   And since He best to love is, and most meek,
What needeth feigned lovës for to seek?
                      Geoffrey Chaucer.

[1] Is not, will not.   [2] Died.

PILGRIMAGE

Give me my scallop-shell of Quiet,
    My staff of Faith to walk upon;
My scrip of Joy, immortal diet,
    My bottle of Salvation,
My gown of Glory, hope's true gage;
And thus I'll take my pilgrimage.

Blood must be my body's balmer,
    No other balm will there be given;
Whilst my soul, like quiet palmer,
    Travelleth towards the land of heaven;
Over the silver mountains,
Where spring the nectar fountains,
        There will I kiss
        The bowl of bliss,
And drink mine everlasting fill
Upon every milken hill.
My soul will be adry before;
But after it will thirst no more.

WRITTEN IN HIS BIBLE THE NIGHT BEFORE HIS EXECUTION

Even such is Time, that takes in trust
    Our youth, our joys, our all we have,

And pays us but with earth and dust;
  Who, in the dark and silent grave,
When we have wandered all our ways,
Shuts up the story of our days ;
But from this earth, this grave, this dust,
My God shall raise me up, I trust !
*   Sir Walter Ralegh.*

THE MINISTRY OF ANGELS

And is there care in heaven? And is there love
  In heavenly spirits to these creatures base,
That may compassion of their evils move?
  There is: else much more wretched were the case
Of men than beasts. But oh, th' exceeding grace
  Of highest God that loves His creatures so,
And all His works with mercy doth embrace,
  That blessed angels He sends to and fro,
To serve to wicked men, to serve His wicked foe.

How oft do they their silver bowers leave
  To come to succour us that succour want!
How oft do they with golden pinions cleave
  The flitting skies, like flying pursuivant,
Against foul fiends to aid us militant!
  They for us fight, they watch and duly ward,
And their bright squadrons round about us plant;
  And all for love, and nothing for reward.
O why should heavenly God to men have such regard?

EASTER DAY

Most glorious Lord of life, that on this day
    Didst make Thy triumph over death and sin,
And, having harrowed hell, didst bring away
    Captivity thence captive, us to win ;
This joyous day, dear Lord, with joy begin,
    And grant that we, for whom Thou diddest die,
Being with Thy dear blood clean washed from sin,
    May live for ever in felicity !
And that Thy love we weighing worthily
    May likewise love Thee for the same again ;
And for Thy sake, that all like dear didst buy,
    With love may one another entertain.
So let us love, dear Love, like as we ought ;
Love is the lesson which the Lord us taught.

THE LOVE OF CHRIST

O huge and most unspeakable impression
    Of love's deep wound, that pierced the piteous heart
Of that dear Lord with so entire affection,
    And, sharply launching[1] every inner part,
    Dolours of death into His soul did dart,

[1] Piercing.

Doing Him die, that never it deserved,
To free His foes, that from His hest had swerved!

What heart can feel least touch of so sore launch,
  Or thought can think the depth of so dear wound?
Whose bleeding source their streams can never staunch,
  But still do flow, and freshly still redound,
  To heal the sores of sinful souls unsound,
  And cleanse the guilt of that infected crime
Which was enrooted in all fleshly slime.

O blessed Well of Love! O Flower of Grace!
  O glorious Morning Star! O Lamp of Light!
Most lively image of Thy Father's face,
  Eternal King of Glory, Lord of Might,
  Meek Lamb of God, before all worlds behight,[1]
  How can we Thee requite for all this good?
Or what can prize[2] that Thy most precious blood?

Yet nought Thou ask'st in lieu of all this love
  But love of us, for guerdon of Thy pain;
Ay me! what can us less than that behove?
  Had He required life of us again,

[1] Ordained.   [2] Equal in value.

Had it been wrong to ask His own with gain?
He gave us life, He it restored, lost;
Then life were least that us so little cost.

But He our life hath left unto us free,
  Free that was thrall, and blessed that was banned;
Ne ought demands but that we loving be,
  As He Himself hath loved us aforehand,
  And bound thereto with an eternal band,
  Him first to love that us so dearly bought,
  And next our brethren, to His image wrought.

Him first to love great right and reason is,
  Who first to us our life and being gave,
And after, when we fared had amiss,
  Us wretches from the second death did save;
  And last, the food of life, which now we have,
  Even He Himself, in His dear sacrament,
  To feed our hungry souls, unto us lent.

Then next to love our brethren, that were made
  Of that self mould and that self Maker's hand
That we, and to the same again shall fade;
  (Where they shall have like heritage of land,
  However here on higher steps we stand)
  Which also were with self-same price redeemed
  That we, however of us light esteemed.

And were they not, yet since that loving Lord
  Commanded us to love them for His sake,
Even for His sake and for His sacred word,
  Which as His last bequest He to us spake,
  We should them love and with their needs partake ;
Knowing that, whatso'er to them we give,
We give to Him by whom we all do live.

Edmund Spenser.

SONNET

Leave me, O love which reachest but to dust,
  And thou, my mind, aspire to higher things,
Grow rich in that which never taketh rust;
  Whatever fades but fading pleasure brings.
Draw in thy beams, and humble all thy might
  To that sweet yoke where lasting freedoms be;
Which breaks the clouds and opens forth the light,
  That doth both shine and give us sight to see.
Oh, take fast hold; let that light be thy guide
  In this small course which birth draws out to death,
And think how ill becometh him to slide
  Who seeketh heaven and comes of heavenly breath.
Then farewell world, thy uttermost I see;
Eternal Love, maintain Thy life in me.

Sir Philip Sidney.

FAITH AND WORKS

Eternal Truth, almighty, infinite,
    Only exilèd from man's fleshly heart,
Where ignorance and disobedience fight
    In hell and sin which shall have greatest part,
When Thy sweet mercy opens forth the light
    Of grace, which giveth eyes unto the blind,
And with the law even plowest up our sprite
    To faith, wherein flesh may salvation find,
Thou bid'st us pray, and we do pray to Thee,
    But as to Power, and God, without us placed,
Thinking a wish may wear out vanity,
    Or habits be by miracles defaced.
One thought to God we give, the rest to sin;
    Quickly unbent is all desire of good;
True words pass out, but have no being within;
    We pray to Christ, yet help to shed His blood;
For while we say *believe*, and feel it not,
    Promise amends, and yet despair in it,
Hear Sodom judged, and go not out with Lot,
    Make law and gospel riddles of the wit,
We with the Jews even Christ still crucify,
    As not yet come to our impiety.

              Fulke Greville, Lord Brooke.

MAN'S CIVIL WAR

My hovering thoughts would fly to heaven,
    And quiet nestle in the sky;
Fain would my ship in Virtue's shore
    Without remove at anchor lie.

But mounting thoughts are haled down,
    With heavy poise of mortal load;
And blustering storms deny my ship
    In Virtue's haven secure abode.

When inward eye to heavenly sights
    Doth draw my longing heart's desire,
The world with jesses of delights
    Would to her perch my thoughts retire.

Fond fancy trains to Pleasure's lure,
    Though Reason stiffly do repine;
Though Wisdom woo me to the saint,
    Yet Sense would win me to the shrine.

Need craves consent of soul to sense,
    Yet divers bents breed civil fray;
Hard hap where halves must disagree,
    Or truce of halves the whole betray!

O cruel fight! where fighting friend
    With love doth kill a favouring foe;
Where peace with sense is war with God,
    And self-delight the seed of woe!

AT HOME IN HEAVEN

Fair soul! how long shall veils thy graces shroud?
How long shall this exile withhold thy right?
When will thy sun disperse his mortal cloud,
    And give thy glories scope to blaze their light?
Oh, that a star, more fit for angels' eyes,
Should pine in earth, not shine above the skies!

Thy ghostly beauty offer'd force to God,
    It chainèd Him in links of tender love;
It won His will with man to make abode;
    It stay'd His sword, and did His wrath remove:
It made the rigour of His justice yield,
And crownèd Mercy empress of the field.

This brought Him from the ranks of heavenly quires
    Into this vale of tears and cursèd soil;
From flowers of grace into a world of briars,
    From life to death, from bliss to baleful toil.
This made Him wander in our pilgrim weed,
And taste our torments to relieve our need.

LOST GRACE

O GRACE, where is the joy
   That makes thy torments sweet?
Where is the cause that many thought
   Their deaths through thee but meet?

Where thy disdain of sin,
   Thy secret, sweet delight?
Thy sparks of bliss, thy heavenly rays,
   That shinèd erst so bright?

O that they were not lost,
   Or I could it excuse;
O that a dream of feignèd loss
   My judgment did abuse!

Yet God's must I remain,
   By death, by wrong, by shame;
I cannot blot out of my heart
   That grace wrought in His name.

I cannot set at nought
   Whom I have held so dear;
I cannot make Him seem afar
   That is indeed so near.

Robert Southwell.

FAITH AND FORM

SACRED Religion, mother of form and fear,
   How gorgeously sometime dost thou sit decked,
What pompous vestures do we make thee wear,
   What stately piles we prodigal erect;
How sweet perfumed thou art, how shining clear,
   How solemnly observed, with what respect!

Another time all plain, all quite threadbare,
   Thou must have all within, and nought without;
Sit poorly, without light, disrobed; no care
   Of outward grace, t'amuse the poor devout;
Powerless, unfollowed, scarcely men can spare
   The necessary rites to set thee out.

WORKS

ALL glory else besides ends with our breath,
   And men's respects scarce bring us to our grave;
But this of doing good must outlive death,
   And have a right out of the right it gave.

Though th' act but few, th' example profiteth
Thousands, that shall thereby a blessing have.
The world's respect grows not but on deserts;
Power may have knees, but Justice hath our
    hearts.

Samuel Daniel.

SELF-KNOWLEDGE

O IGNORANT poor man! what dost thou bear,
   Locked up within the casket of thy breast?
What jewels and what riches hast thou here!
   What heavenly treasure in so weak a chest!

Think of her worth and think that God did mean
   This worthy mind should worthy things embrace:
Blot not her beauties with thy thoughts unclean,
   Nor her dishonour with thy passion base.

Kill not her quickening power with surfeitings;
   Mar not her sense with sensuality;
Cast not her serious wit on idle things;
   Make not her free-will slave to vanity.

And when thou think'st of her eternity,
   Think not that death against her nature is;
Think it a birth; and when thou go'st to die,
   Sing like a swan, as if thou went'st to bliss.

And thou my soul, which turn'st thy curious eye
  To view the beams of thine own form divine,
Know, that thou can'st know nothing perfectly,
  While thou art clouded with this flesh of mine.

Cast down thyself and only strive to raise
  The glory of thy Maker's sacred name:
Use all thy powers that blessed Power to praise,
  Which gives thee power to be and use the same.

SELF-IGNORANCE

We seek to know the moving of each sphere,
  And the strange cause of th' ebbs and flouds of Nile;
But of that clock within our breasts we bear,
  The subtle motions we forget the while.

We that acquaint ourselves with every zone
  And pass both tropics, and behold the poles,
When we come home are to ourselves unknown,
  And unacquainted still with our own souls.
Sir John Davies.

THE CHARACTER OF A HAPPY LIFE

How happy is he born and taught
   That serveth not another's will;
Whose armour is his honest thought,
   And simple truth his utmost skill;

Whose passions not his masters are;
   Whose soul is still prepared for death,
Untied unto the world by care
   Of public fame or private breath;

Who envies none that chance doth raise,
   Nor vice; who never understood
How deepest wounds are given by praise;
   Nor rules of state, but rules of good;

Who hath his life from rumours freed;
   Whose conscience is his strong retreat;
Whose state can neither flatterers feed,
   Nor ruin make oppressors great;

Who God doth late and early pray
   More of His grace than gifts to lend;
And entertains the harmless day
   With a religious book or friend.

This man is freed from servile bands
  Of hope to rise or fear to fall :
Lord of himself, though not of lands,
  And, having nothing, yet hath all.

HYMN

ETERNAL Mover, whose diffusèd glory,
  To show our grovelling reason what Thou art,
Unfolds itself in clouds of nature's story,
  Where man, Thy proudest creature, acts his part,
Whom yet, alas, I know not why, we call
The world's contracted sum, the little all ;

For what are we but lumps of walking clay?
  Why should we swell? whence should our spirits rise?
Are not brute beasts as strong, and birds as gay,—
  Trees longer-lived, and creeping things as wise?
Only our souls were left an inward light,
To feel our weakness, and confess Thy might.

Thou then, our strength, Father of life and death,
  To whom our thanks, our vows, ourselves we owe,

From me, Thy tenant of this fading breath,
   Accept those lines which from Thy goodness
      flow,
And Thou, that wert Thy regal Prophet's muse,
Do not Thy praise in weaker strains refuse!

Let these poor notes ascend unto Thy throne,
   Where majesty doth sit with mercy crowned,
Where my Redeemer lives, in whom alone
   The errors of my wandering life are drowned :
Where all the choir of heaven resound the
      same,
That only Thine, Thine is the saving name!

Well then, my soul, joy in the midst of pain;
   Thy Christ, that conquered hell, shall from
      above
With greater triumph yet return again,
   And conquer His own justice with His love;
Commanding earth and seas to render those
Unto His bliss, for whom He paid His woes.

Now have I done; now are my thoughts at
      peace;
   And now my joys are stronger than my grief:
I feel those comforts, that shall never cease,
   Future in hope, but present in belief:
Thy words are true, Thy promises are just,
And Thou wilt find Thy dearly-bought in dust!

A HYMN TO MY GOD

O Thou Great Power ! in whom I move,
   For whom I live, to whom I die,
Behold me through Thy beams of love,
   Whilst on this couch of tears I lie ;
And cleanse my sordid soul within
By Thy Christ's blood, the bath of sin !

No hallowed oils, no grains I need,
   No rags of saints, no purging fire ;
One rosy drop from David's seed
   Was worlds of seas to quench Thine ire.
O precious ransom ! which once paid,
That *consummatum est* was said :

And said by Him that said no more,
   But sealed it with His sacred breath :
Thou, then, that hast dispunged my score,
   And dying wast the death of Death,
Be to me now, on Thee I call,
My life, my strength, my joy, my all !
                   Sir Henry Wotton.

FOUR SONNETS

I.

Thou hast made me, and shall Thy work decay?
  Repair me now; for now mine end doth haste,
  I run to Death, and Death meets me as fast,
And all my pleasures are like yesterday.

I dare not move my dim eyes any way,
  Despair behind and Death before doth cast
  Such terror, and my feeble flesh doth waste
By sin in it, which it towards Hell doth weigh.

Only Thou art above, and when towards Thee
  By Thy leave I can look, I rise again;
But our old subtle foe so tempteth me,
  That not one hour myself I can sustain.

Thy grace may wing me to prevent his art,
And Thou like adamant[1] draw mine iron heart.

II.

As due by many titles, I resign
Myself to Thee, O God! First I was made

[1] Magnet.

By Thee and for Thee ; and when I was decay'd,
Thy blood bought that, the which before was
    Thine.
I am Thy son, made with Thyself to shine ;
Thy servant, whose pains Thou hast still re-
    paid ;
Thy sheep, Thine image ; and till I betray'd
Myself, a temple of Thy Spirit Divine.
Why doth the devil then usurp on me ?
Why doth he steal, nay, ravish that's Thy right ?
Except Thou rise and for Thine own work fight,
Oh, I shall soon despair, when I shall see
That Thou lov'st mankind well, yet wilt not
    choose me,
And Satan hates me yet is loth to lose me.

III.

At the round earth's imagin'd corners blow
Your trumpets, angels ; and arise, arise
From death, you numberless infinities
Of souls, and to your scattered bodies go,
All whom th' flood did, and fire shall over
    throw ;
All whom war, death, age, ague's tyrannies,
Despair, law, chance, hath slain ; and you
    whose eyes
Shall behold God and never taste death's woe.
But let them sleep, Lord, and me mourn a
    space ;

For if above all these my sins abound,
'Tis late to ask abundance of Thy grace
When we are there. Here on this holy ground
Teach me how to repent, for that's as good
As if Thou hadst sealed my pardon with Thy blood.

IV.

Death, be not proud, though some have called thee
Mighty and dreadful, for thou art not so;
For those whom thou think'st thou dost overthrow
Die not, poor Death! nor yet canst thou kill me.
From rest and sleep, which but thy picture be,
Much pleasure, then from thee much more must flow;
And soonest our best men with thee do go,
Rest of their bones, and soul's delivery.
Thou'rt slave to fate, chance, kings, and desperate men,
And dost with poison, war, and sickness dwell;
And poppy or charms can make us sleep as well
And better than thy stroke. Why swell'st thou then?
One short sleep past, we wake eternally;
And Death shall be no more; Death, thou shalt die!

LITANY

FATHER of heav'n, and Him by whom
It, and us for it, and all else for us,
Thou mad'st and govern'st ever ; come,
And re-create me, now grown ruinous ;
My heart is by dejection clay,
And by self-murder red.
From this red earth, O Father, purge away
All vicious tinctures, that new-fashioned
I may rise up from death before I'm dead.

O Son of God, who seeing two things,
Sin and death, crept in which were never made ;
By bearing one, tri'dst with what stings
The other could Thine heritage invade ;
O be Thou nail'd unto my heart,
And crucified again.
Part not from it, though it from Thee would part,
But let it be, by applying so Thy pain,
Drown'd in Thy blood, and in Thy passion slain.

O Holy Ghost, whose temple I
Am, but of mud walls and condensed dust,
And being sacrilegiously
Half wasted with youth's fires of pride and lust,
Must with new storms be weather-beat ;
Double in my heart Thy flame,

Which let devout sad tears intend, and let
(Though this glass lanthorn flesh do suffer
    maim)
Fire, sacrifice, priest, altar, be the same.

A HYMN TO GOD THE FATHER

WILT Thou forgive that sin where I begun,
    Which was my sin, though it were done
      before?
Wilt Thou forgive that sin through which I run
    And do run still, though still I do deplore?
      When Thou hast done, Thou hast not done;
        For I have more.

Wilt Thou forgive that sin which I have won
    Others to sin, and made my sins their door?
Wilt Thou forgive that sin which I did shun
    A year or two, but wallow'd in a score?
      When Thou hast done, Thou hast not done;
        For I have more.

I have a sin of fear, that when I have spun
    My last thread, I shall perish on the shore;
But swear by Thyself, that at my death Thy
    Son
    Shall shine, as He shines now and hereto-
      fore;
    And having done that, Thou hast done;
        I fear no more.

HYMN TO GOD
IN MY SICKNESS

Since I am coming to that holy room,
Where with the choir of saints for evermore
I shall be made Thy music, as I come
I tune the instrument here at the door,
And what I must do then, think here before.

We think that Paradise and Calvary,
Christ's cross and Adam's tree, stood in one
    place;
Look, Lord, and find both Adams met in me;
As the first Adam's sweat surrounds my face,
May the last Adam's blood my soul embrace.

So in His purple wrapp'd receive me, Lord,
By these His thorns give me His other crown;
And as to other souls I preach'd Thy word,
Be this my text, my sermon to mine own:
" Therefore, that He may raise, the Lord
    throws down."

GOOD FRIDAY
RIDING WESTWARD

Hence is't that I am carried towards the west,
This day, when my soul's form bends to the
    east;

Yet dare I almost be glad I do not see
That spectacle of too much weight for me.
Who sees God's face, that is self-life, must die;
What a death were it then to see God die!
It made His own lieutenant, Nature, shrink;
It made His footstool crack, and the sun wink.
Could I behold those hands which span the poles
And tune all spheres at once, pierced with those holes?
Could I behold that endless height, which is
Zenith to us and our Antipodes,
Humbled below us? or that blood, which is
The seat of all our souls, if not of His,
Made dirt of dust? or that flesh, which was worn
By God for His apparel, ragg'd and torn?
Though these things as I ride be from mine eye,
They're present yet unto my memory;
For that looks toward them, and Thou look'st towards me
O Saviour, as Thou hang'st upon the tree.
I turn my back to Thee but to receive
Corrections; till Thy mercies bid Thee leave.
O think me worth Thine anger, punish me,
Burn off my rust and my deformity;
Restore Thine image so much by Thy grace,
That Thou may'st know me, and I'll turn my face.

EASTER DAY

Sleep, sleep, old Sun! thou canst not have repast
As yet the wound thou took'st on Friday last;
Sleep then and rest; the world may bear thy stay,
A better sun rose before thee to-day.
Who not content t' enlighten all that dwell
On the earth's face, as thou, enlighten'd hell;
And made the dark fires languish in that vale,
As at thy presence here our fires grow pale.
Whose body, having walk'd on earth, and now
Hastening to heaven, would—that He might allow
Himself unto all stations, and fill all—
For these three days become a mineral.
He was all gold when He lay down, but rose
All tincture, and doth not alone dispose
Leaden and iron wills to good, but is
Of power to make ev'n sinful flesh like His.

THE CROSS

Since Christ embraced the Cross itself, dare I,
His image, th' image of His Cross deny?
Would I have profit by the sacrifice,
And dare the chosen altar to despise?

It bore all other sins, but is it fit
That it should bear the sin of scorning it?
Who from the picture would avert his eye,
How would he fly His pains who there did die?
From me no pulpit, nor misgrounded law,
Nor scandal taken, shall this cross withdraw.

CHRIST THE JUDGE

WHAT if this present were the world's last night?
Mark in my heart, O Soul, where thou dost dwell,
The picture of Christ crucified, and tell
Whether His countenance can thee affright?
Tears in His eyes quench the amazing light;
Blood fills His frowns which from His pierced head fell.
And can that tongue adjudge thee unto hell
Which prayed forgiveness for His foes' fierce spite?

CROSSES

As perchance carvers do not faces make,
But that away which hid them there do take;
Let crosses so take what hid Christ in thee,
And be His image, or not His, but He.

Dean John Donne.

AN HYMN TO GOD THE FATHER

Hear me, O God!
   A broken heart
   Is my best part:
Use still Thy rod,
   That I may prove
   Therein Thy love.

If Thou hadst not
   Been stern to me,
   But left me free,
I had forgot
   Myself and Thee.

For sin's so sweet,
   As minds ill bent
   Rarely repent,
Until they meet
   Their punishment.

Who more can crave
   Than Thou hast done?
   Thou gav'st a Son
To free a slave:
   First made of nought,
   Withal since bought.

Sin, death, and hell
  His glorious name
  Quite overcame;
Yet I rebel,
  And slight the same.

But I'll come in
  Before my loss
  Me farther toss,
As sure to win
  Under His cross.

TO HEAVEN

Good and great God! can I not think of Thee
But it must straight my melancholy be?
Is it interpreted in me disease,
That laden with my sins I seek for ease?
O, be Thou witness, that the reins dost know
And hearts of all, if I be sad for show;
And judge me after if I dare pretend
To aught but grace, or aim at other end.
As Thou art all, so be Thou all to me,
First, midst, and last, converted one and three,
My faith, my hope, my love; and in this state
My judge, my witness, and my advocate.
Where have I been this while exiled from Thee?
And whither rapt, now Thou but stoop'st to
  me?

Dwell, dwell here still; O, being everywhere
How can I doubt to find Thee ever here?
I know my state, both full of shame and scorn,
Conceived in sin, and unto labour born;
Standing with fear, and must with horror fall,
And destined unto judgment after all.
I feel my griefs too, and there scarce is ground
Upon my flesh to inflict another wound.
Yet dare I not complain or wish for death
With holy Paul, lest it be thought the breath
Of discontent: or that these prayers be
For weariness of life, not love of Thee.

THE FORTRESS OF MANSOUL

Not to know vice at all, and keep true state,
    Is virtue and not fate:
Next to that virtue is to know vice well,
    And her black spite repel.
Which to effect (since no breast is so sure,
    Or safe, but she'll procure
Some way of entrance), we must plant a guard
    Of thoughts to watch and ward
At th' eye and ear, the ports unto the mind,
    That no strange or unkind
Object arrive there, but the heart, our spy,
    Give knowledge instantly
To wakeful reason, our affections' king:
    Who in th' examining

Will quickly taste the treason, and commit
    Close the true cause of it.
'Tis the securest policy we have
    To make our sense our slave.
But this true course is not embraced by many ;
    By many? scarce by any.
For either our affections do rebel,
    Or else the sentinel,
That should ring 'larum to the heart, doth sleep,
    Or some great thought doth keep
Back the intelligence, and falsely swears
    They're base and idle fears
Whereof the loyal conscience so complains.
    Thus by these subtle trains
Do several passions invade the mind
    And strike our reason blind.

Ben Jonson.

A HYMN OF THE RESURRECTION

Life out of death, light out of darkness springs,
From a base jail forth comes the King of kings.
What late was mortal, thrall'd to every woe
That lackeys life, or upon sense doth grow,
Immortal is of an eternal stamp,
Far brighter beaming than the morning lamp:
So from a black eclipse outpeers the sun:
Such (when her course of days have on her run
In a far forest in the pearly east,
And she herself hath burnt her spicy nest)
The lonely bird with youthful pens and comb,
Doth soar from out her cradle and her tomb:
So a small seed that in the earth lies hid
And dies, reviving bursts her cloddy side,
Adorn'd with yellow locks of new is born,
And doth become a mother great with corn,
Of grains brings hundreds with it, which when old
Enrich the furrows with a sea of gold.

FAITH WITHOUT WORKS

As body when the soul has fled,
As barren trees decayed and dead,
Is faith, a hopeless lifeless thing,
If not of righteous deeds the spring.

One cup of healing oil and wine,
One tear-drop shed on Mercy's shrine,
Is thrice more grateful, Lord, to Thee,
Than lifted eye or bended knee.

CHANGE SHOULD BREED CHANGE

New doth the sun appear;
The mountains' snows decay;
Crowned with frail flowers comes forth the baby year.
My soul, time posts away;
And thou yet in that frost,
Which flower and fruit hath lost,
As if all here immortal were, dost stay!

William Drummond.

LITANY

In the hour of my distress,
When temptations me oppress,
And when I my sins confess,
      Sweet Spirit, comfort me!

When I lie within my bed,
Sick in heart and sick in head,
And with doubts discomforted,
      Sweet Spirit, comfort me!

When the house doth sigh and weep,
And the world is drown'd in sleep,
Yet mine eyes the watch do keep,
      Sweet Spirit, comfort me!

When the passing bell doth toll,
And the furies in a shoal
Come to fright a parting soul,
      Sweet Spirit, comfort me!

When the tapers now burn blue,
And the comforters are few,
And that number more than true,
      Sweet Spirit, comfort me!

When the priest his last hath prayed,
And I nod to what is said,
'Cause my speech is now decayed,
    Sweet Spirit, comfort me!

When, God knows, I'm toss'd about,
Either with despair or doubt;
Yet, before the glass be out,
    Sweet Spirit, comfort me!

When the tempter me pursu'th
With the sins of all my youth,
And half damns me with untruth,
    Sweet Spirit, comfort me!

When the flames and hellish cries
Fright mine ears, and fright mine eyes,
And all terrors me surprise,
    Sweet Spirit, comfort me!

When the judgment is reveal'd,
And that open'd which was seal'd,
When to Thee I have appeal'd,
    Sweet Spirit, comfort me!

ETERNITY

O YEARS! and age! farewell:
    Behold, I go
    Where I do know
Infinity to dwell.

And these mine eyes shall see
      All times, how they
      Are lost i' th' sea
Of vast eternity.

Where never moon shall sway
      The stars; but she
      And night shall be
Drown'd in one endless day.

TO HIS CONSCIENCE

Can I not sin, but thou wilt be
My private protonotary?[1]
Can I not woo thee to pass by
A short and sweet iniquity?
I'll cast a mist and cloud upon
My delicate transgression,
So utter dark as that no eye
Shall see the hugg'd impiety;
Gifts blind the wise, and bribes do please
And wind all other witnesses;
And wilt not thou with gold be ti'd
To lay thy pen and ink aside?
It will not be. And, therefore, now,
For times to come I'll make this vow,
From aberrations to live free;
So I'll not fear the Judge or thee.

[1] Chief Clerk of the High Court.

LENT

Is this a fast, to keep
  The larder lean?
   And clean
From fat of veals and sheep?

Is it to quit the dish
  Of flesh, yet still
   To fill
The platter high with fish?

Is it to fast an hour,
  Or ragg'd to go?
   Or show
A downcast look and sour?

No; 'tis a fast to dole
  Thy sheaf of wheat,
   And meat,
Unto the hungry soul.

It is to fast from strife,
  From old debate
   And hate;
To circumcise thy life.

To show a heart grief-rent;
  To starve thy sin,
   Not bin;
And that's to keep thy Lent.

TO DEATH

Thou bid'st me come away,
And I'll no longer stay
Than for to shed some tears
For faults of former years,
And to repent some crimes
Done in the present times:
And next, to take a bit
Of bread, and wine with it:
To don my robes of love,
Fit for the place above;
To gird my loins about
With charity throughout;
And so to travel hence
With feet of innocence:
These done, I'll only cry
God mercy, and so die.

TO FIND GOD

Weigh me the fire; or can'st thou find
A way to measure out the wind;
Distinguish all those floods that are
Mix'd in that watery theatre;
And taste thou them as saltless there
As in their channel first they were.
Tell me the people that do keep
Within the kingdoms of the deep;

Or fetch me back that cloud again,
Beshiver'd into seeds of rain;
Tell me the motes, dust, sands, and spears
Of corn, when summer shakes his ears;
Show me that world of stars, and whence
They noiseless spill their influence:
This if thou canst, then show me Him
That rides the glorious cherubim.

UPON GOD

God, when He takes my goods and chattels hence,
Gives me a portion, giving patience:
What is in God is God; if so it be,
He patience gives, He gives Himself to me.

HUMILITY

Humble we must be, if to heaven we go:
High is the roof there; but the gate is low.
Robert Herrick.

THE INCARNATION

What hath man done, that man shall not undo,
Since God to him is grown so near akin!
Did his foe slay him? he shall slay his foe:
Hath he lost all? he all again shall win:
Is sin his master? he shall master sin:
    Too hardy soul, with sin the field to try:
    The only way to conquer, was to fly;
But thus long death hath lived, and now death's
    self shall die.

He is a path, if any be misled;
He is a robe, if any naked be;
If any chance to hunger, He is bread;
If any be a bondman, He is free;
If any be but weak, how strong is He?
    To dead men life He is, to sick men health:
    To blind men sight, and to the needy
        wealth;
A pleasure without loss, a treasure without
    stealth.

Who can forget, never to be forgot,
The time that all the world in slumber lies:
When, like the stars, the singing angels shot
To earth, and heav'n awaked all his eyes,

To see another sun at midnight rise
    On earth? was never sight of pareil fame:
    For God before, man like Himself did frame,
But God Himself now like a mortal man became.

A child He was, and had not learned to speak,
That with His word the world before did make:
His mother's arms Him bore, he was so weak,
That with one hand the vaults of heav'n could
    shake.
See how small room my infant Lord doth take,
    Whom all the world is not enough to hold.
    Who of His years, or of His age hath told?
Never such age so young, never a child so old.

And yet but newly He was infanted,
And yet already He was sought to die;
Yet scarcely born, already banished;
Not able yet to go, and forced to fly:
But scarcely fled away, when by and by,
    The tyrant's sword with blood is all defil'd,
    And Rachel for her sons, with fury wild,
Cries, O thou cruel king, and O my sweetest
    child!

Egypt his nurse became, where Nilus springs,
Who straight, to entertain the rising sun,
The hasty harvest in his bosom brings;
But now for drought the fields were all undone,

And now with waters all is overrun :
    So fast the Cynthian mountains pour'd
      their snow,
    When once they felt the sun so near them
      glow,
That Nilus Egypt lost, and to a sea did grow.

The angels caroll'd loud their song of peace,
The cursed oracles were strucken dumb ;
To see their Shepherd the poor shepherds press,
To see their king the kingly sophies come ;
And them to guide unto his Master's home,
    A star comes dancing up the orient,
    That springs for joy over the strawy tent,
Where gold, to make their prince a crown, they
    all present.

THE PASSION

FRAIL multitude ! whose giddy law is list,[1]
And best applause is windy flattering,
Most like the breath of which it doth consist,
No sooner blown but as soon vanishing,
As much desired, as little profiting,
    That makes the men that have it oft as
      light
    As those that give it, which the proud
      invite,
And fear ; the bad man's friend, the good man's
    hypocrite.

[1] Lust, desire.

It was but now their sounding clamours sung,
"Blessed is He that comes from the Most
    High!"
And all the mountains with hosannah rung;
And now, "Away with Him, away!" they
    cry,
And nothing can be heard but "Crucify":
    It was but now the crown itself they save,
      And golden name of King unto Him gave;
And now no king but only Cæsar they will
    have.

It was but now they gathered blooming May,
And of his arms disrobed the branching tree,
To strow with boughs and blossoms all Thy
    way;
And now the branchless trunk a cross for Thee,
And May, dismay'd, thy coronet must be:
    It was but now they were so kind to throw
      Their own best garments, where Thy feet
        should go;
And now Thyself they strip, and bleeding
    wounds they show.

See where the Author of all life is dying:
O fearful day! He dead, what hope of living?
See where the hopes of all our lives are buy-
    ing;
O cheerful day! they bought, what fear of
    grieving?

Love love for hate and life for death is giving:
    Lo, how His arms are stretch'd abroad to grace thee,
    And, as they open stand, call to embrace thee:
Why stay'st thou then, my soul? O fly, fly, thither haste thee!

What better friendship than to cover shame?
What greater love than for a friend to die?
Yet this is better to asself[1] the blame,
And this is greater, for an enemy:
But more than this, to die, not suddenly,
    Not with some common death or easy pain,
    But slowly, and with torments to be slain:
O depth without a depth, far better seen than say'n!

And yet the Son is humbled for the slave,
And yet the slave is proud before the Son:
Yet the Creator for His creature gave
Himself, and yet the creature hastes to run
From his Creator, and self-good doth shun:
    And yet the Prince, and God Himself, doth cry
    To man, his traitor, pardon not to fly:
Yet man his God, and traitor doth his Prince defy.

[1] Take on oneself.

THE RESURRECTION

But now the second morning from her bow'r
Began to glister in her beams, and now
The roses of the day began to flow'r
In th' eastern garden; for heav'n's smiling brow
Half insolent for joy, began to show;
    The early sun came lively dancing out,
    And the brag lambs ran wantoning about,
That heav'n and earth might seem in triumph
    both to shout.

Say, earth, why hast thou got thee new attire,
And stick'st thy habit full of daisies red!
Seems that thou dost to some high thought
    aspire,
And some new-found-out bridegroom mean'st
    to wed:
Tell me, ye trees, so fresh apparelled,—
    So never let the spiteful canker waste you,
    So never let the heav'ns with lightning
        blast you,—
Why go you now so trimly drest, or whither
    haste you?

Answer me, Jordan, why thy crooked tide
So often wanders from his nearest way,
As though some other way thy stream would
    slide,
And fain salute the place where something lay.

And you, sweet birds, that shaded from the ray,
    Sit carolling and piping grief away,
        The while the lambs to hear you dance and play,
Tell me, sweet birds, what is it you so fain would say?

Ye primroses and purple violets,
Tell me, why blaze ye from your leavy beds,
And woo men's hands to rend you from your sets,
As though you would somewhere be carried,
With fresh perfumes, and velvets garnished?
    But ah! I need not ask, 'tis surely so,
    You all would to your Saviour's triumph go,
There would ye all await, and humble homage do.

EARTH AND HEAVEN

Gaze but upon the house where man embow'rs:
With flow'rs and rushes paved is his way,
Where all the creatures are his servitors,
The winds do sweep his chambers every day,
And clouds do wash his rooms, the ceiling gay
    Starred aloft the gilded knobs embrave:
    If such a house God to another gave,
How shine those glittering courts He for Himself will have!

And if a sullen cloud, as sad as night,
In which the sun may seem embodied,
Depur'd of all his dross we see so white,
Burning in melted gold his watery head,
Or round with ivory edges silvered :
  What lustre super-excellent will HE
  Lighten on those that shall His sunshine see,
In that all-glorious court in which all glories be ?
Giles Fletcher.

FROM "THE CHURCH PORCH"

EDUCATION

O ENGLAND! full of sin, but most of sloth;
Spit out thy phlegm, and fill thy breast with glory;
Thy gentry bleats, as if thy native cloth
Transfus'd a sheepishness into thy story.
   Not that they all are so; but that the most
   Are gone to grass, and in the pasture lost.

This loss springs chiefly from our education.
Some till their ground, but let weeds choke their son:
Some mark a partridge, never their child's fashion;
Some ship them over, and the thing is done.
   Study this art, and make it thy great design;
   And if God's image move thee not, let thine.

Some great estates provide, but do not breed
A mast'ring mind; so both are lost thereby:
Or else they breed them tender, make them need
All that they leave: this is flat poverty,
   For he that needs five thousand pound to live
   Is full as poor as he that needs but five.

WEALTH

Be thrifty, but not covetous: therefore give
Thy need, thine honour, and thy friend his due.
Never was scraper brave man. Get to live;
Then live and use it: else it is not true
    That thou hast gotten. Surely use alone
    Makes money not a contemptible stone.

What skills it, if a bag of stones or gold
About thy neck do drown thee? raise thy head.
Take stars for money; stars not to be told
By any art, yet to be purchased.
    None is so wasteful as the scraping dame.
    She loseth three for one; her soul, rest, fame.

FRIENDSHIP

Thy friend put in thy bosom: wear his eyes
Still in thy heart, that he may see what's there.
If cause require, thou art his sacrifice;
Thy drops of blood must pay down all his fear;
    But love is lost; the way of friendship's gone,
    Though David had his Jonathan, Christ His
        John.

Yet be not surety, if thou be a father.
Love is a personal debt. I cannot give

My children's right, nor ought he take it: rather
Both friends should die, than hinder them to
    live :
  Fathers first enter bonds to nature's ends ;
  And are her sureties, ere they are a friend's.

CONDUCT

When thou dost purpose aught, within thy
    power,
Be sure to do it, though it be but small :
Constancy knits the bones, and make us stour[1]
When wanton pleasures beckon us to thrall.
  Who breaks his own bond, forfeiteth himself:
  What nature made a ship, he makes a shelf.

Pitch thy behaviour low, thy projects high ;
So shalt thou humble and magnanimous be :
Sink not in spirit : who aimeth at the sky,
Shoots higher much than he that means a tree.
  A grain of glory mixed with humbleness
  Cures both a fever and lethargickness.

By all means use sometimes to be alone.
Salute thyself : see what thy soul doth wear.
Dare to look in thy chest, for 'tis thine own,
And tumble up and down what thou find'st
    there.
  Who cannot rest till he good fellows find,
  He breaks up house, turns out of doors his
      mind.

[1] Sturdy.

HEALTH

Slight those who say amidst their sickly
    healths,
Thou liv'st by rule. What doth not so but
    man?
Houses are built by rule, and commonwealths.
Entice the trusty sun, if that you can,
    From his ecliptic line; beckon the sky.
    Who lives by rule then keeps good company.

Who keeps no guard upon himself is slack,
And rots to nothing at the next great thaw.
Man is a shop of rules, a well-truss'd pack,
Whose every parcel under-writes a law.
    Lose not thyself, nor give thy humours way;
    God gave them to thee under lock and key.

MATTENS

    I cannot ope mine eyes,
  But Thou art ready there to catch
  My morning-soul and sacrifice:
Then we must needs for that day make a match.

    My God, what is a heart?
  Silver, or gold, or precious stone,
  Or star, or rainbow, or a part
Of all these things or all of them in one?

My God, what is a heart,
That Thou should'st it so eye, and woo,
Pouring upon it all Thy art,
As if that Thou hadst nothing else to do?

Indeed man's whole estate
Amounts (and richly) to serve Thee:
He did not heav'n and earth create,
Yet studies them, not Him by whom they be.

Teach me Thy love to know;
That this new light, which now I see,
May both the work and Workman show:
Then by a sunbeam I will climb to Thee.

PRAISE

King of Glory, King of Peace,
    I will love Thee:
And that love may never cease,
    I will move Thee.

Thou hast granted my request,
    Thou hast heard me:
Thou didst note my working breast,
    Thou hast spar'd me.

Wherefore with my utmost art
    I will sing Thee,
And the cream of all my heart
    I will bring Thee.

Though my sins against me cried,
    Thou didst clear me;
And alone, when they replied,
    Thou didst hear me.

Sev'n whole days, not one in seven,
    I will praise Thee.
In my heart, though not in heaven,
    I can raise Thee.

Thou grew'st soft and moist with tears,
    Thou relentedst:
And when Justice call'd for fears,
    Thou dissentedst.

Small it is, in this poor sort
    To enrol Thee,
Ev'n eternity is too short
    To extol Thee.

SIN

Lord, with what care hast Thou begirt us round!
  Parents first season us: then schoolmasters
  Deliver us to laws; they send us bound
To rules of reason, holy messengers,

Pulpits and Sundays, sorrow dogging sin,
   Afflictions sorted, anguish of all sizes,
   Fine nets and stratagems to catch us in,
Bibles laid open, millions of surprises,

Blessings beforehand, ties of gratefulness,
   The sound of glory ringing in our ears.
   Without, our shame; within, our consciences;
Angels and grace, eternal hopes and fears.

   Yet all these fences and their whole array
   One cunning bosom-sin blows quite away.

THE PEARL

I KNOW the ways of learning; both the head
And pipes that feed the press, and make it run;
What reason hath from nature borrowed,
Or of itself, like a good housewife, spun
In laws and policy; what the stars conspire,
What willing nature speaks, what forced by
    fire;
Both th' old discoveries, and the new-found seas;
The stock and surplus, cause and history:
All these stand open, or I have the keys:
          Yet I love Thee.

I know the ways of honour, what maintains
The quick returns of courtesy and wit:
In vies of favours whether party gains,
When glory swells the heart, and mouldeth it

To all expressions both of hand and eye,
Which on the world a true love-knot may tie,
And bear the bundle wheresoe'er it goes:
How many drams of spirit there must be
To sell my life unto my friends or foes:
    Yet I love Thee.

I know the ways of pleasure, the sweet strains,
The lullings and the relishes of it;
The propositions of hot blood and brains;
What mirth and music mean; what love and
  wit
Have done these twenty hundred years, and
  more:
I know the projects of unbridled store:
My stuff is flesh, not brass; my senses live,
And grumble oft, that they have more in me
Than he that curbs them, being but one to five;
    Yet I love Thee.

I know all these, and have them in my hand:
Therefore not sealed, but with open eyes
I fly to thee, and fully understand
Both the main sale, and the commodities;
And at what rate and price I have Thy love;
With all the circumstances that may move:
Yet through the labyrinths, not my grovelling
  wit,
But Thy silk twist let down from heav'n to me,
Did both conduct and teach me, how by it
    To climb to Thee.

THE PULLEY

    When God at first made man,
Having a glass of blessings standing by;
Let us (said He) pour on him all we can:
Let the world's riches, which dispersed lie,
        Contract into a span.

    So strength first made a way;
Then beauty flow'd, then wisdom, honour, pleasure:
When almost all was out, God made a stay,
Perceiving that alone of all His treasure
        Rest in the bottom lay.

    For if I should (said He)
Bestow this jewel also on my creature,
He would adore My gifts instead of Me,
And rest in Nature, not the God of Nature.
        So both should losers be.

    Yet let him keep the rest,
But keep them with repining restlessness:
Let him be rich and weary, that at least
If goodness lead him not, yet weariness
        May toss him to My breast.

MAN'S MEDLEY

Hark, how the birds do sing,
    And woods do ring.
All creatures have their joy : and man hath his.
    Yet if we rightly measure,
      Man's joy and pleasure
Rather hereafter, than in present, is.

To this life things of sense
    Make their pretence ;
In th' other angels have a right by birth :
    Man ties them both alone,
      And makes them one,
With th' one hand touching heav'n, with th' other earth.

In soul he mounts and flies,
    In flesh he dies,
He wears a stuff whose thread is coarse and round,
    But trimm'd with curious lace,
      And should take place,
After the trimming not the stuff and ground.

Not that he may not here
    Taste of the cheer,

But as birds drink, and straight lift up their
    head,
        So must he sip and think
            Of better drink
He may attain to after he is dead.

        But as his joys are double,
            So is his trouble.
He hath two winters, other things but one ;
        Both frosts and thoughts do nip,
            And bite his lip ;
And he of all things fears two deaths alone.

        Yet ev'n the greatest griefs
            May be reliefs,
Could he but take them right, and in their ways.
        Happy is he, whose heart
            Hath found the art
To turn his double pains to double praise.

THE QUIP

THE merry world did on a day
With his train-bands and mates agree
To meet together, where I lay,
And all in sport to jeer at me.

First, Beauty crept into a rose,
Which, when I pluck'd not, Sir, said she,
Tell me, I pray, whose hands are those ?
But Thou shalt answer, Lord, for me.

Then Money came, and chinking still,
What tune is this, poor man? said he:
I heard in Music you had skill.
But Thou shalt answer, Lord, for me.

Then came brave [1] Glory puffing by
In silks that whistled, who but he?
He scarce allow'd me half an eye.
But Thou shalt answer, Lord, for me.

Then came quick Wit and Conversation,
And he would needs a comfort be,
And, to be short, make an oration.
But Thou shalt answer, Lord, for me.

Yet when the hour of Thy design
To answer these fine things shall come;
Speak not at large, say, I am Thine:
And then they have their answer home.

THE COLLAR

I struck the board, and cry'd, No more.
        I will abroad.
What? shall I ever sigh and pine?
My lines and life are free; free as the road,
  Loose as the wind, as large as store.
       Shall I be still in suit?
Have I no harvest but a thorn
To let me blood, and not restore

[1] Finely drest.

What I have lost with cordial fruit?
    Sure there was wine
  Before my sighs did dry it : there was corn
  Before my tears did drown it.
 Is the year only lost to me?
  Have I no bays to crown it?
No flowers, no garlands gay? all blasted?
    All wasted?
 Not so, my heart : but there is fruit,
   And thou hast hands.
 Recover all thy sigh-blown age
On double pleasures : leave thy cold dispute
Of what is fit and not : forsake thy cage,
   Thy rope of sands,
Which petty thoughts have made, and made to thee
  Good cable, to enforce and draw,
    And be thy law,
 While thou didst wink[1] and wouldst not see.
   Away; take heed:
   I will abroad.
Call in thy death's head there : tie up thy fears.
   He that forbears,
  To suit and serve his need,
   Deserves his load.
But as I raved and grew more fierce and wild
   At every word,
 Methought I heard one calling, *Child*:
  And I replied, *My Lord*.

[1] Shut eyes.

THE PILGRIMAGE

I travell'd on, seeing the hill, where lay
      My expectation.
   A long it was and weary way.
    The gloomy cave of Desperation
I left on th' one, and on the other side
      The rock of Pride.

And so I came to Fancy's meadow strow'd
      With many a flower:
   Fain would I here have made abode,
   But I was quicken'd by my hour.
So to Care's copse I came, and there got through
      With much ado.

That led me to the wild of Passion, which
      Some call the wold;
   A wasted place, but sometimes rich.
   Here I was robb'd of all my gold,
Save one good Angel, which a friend had tied
      Close to my side.

At length I got unto the gladsome hill,
      Where lay my hope,
   Where lay my heart; and climbing still,
   When I had gain'd the brow and top,
A lake of brackish waters on the ground
      Was all I found.

With that abash'd and struck with many a sting
      Of swarming fears,
  I fell, and cried, Alas, my King;
   Can both the way and end be tears?
Yet taking heart I rose, and then perceived
      I was deceived:

My hill was further; so I flung away,
      Yet heard a cry
  Just as I went, *None goes that way
  And lives.* If that be all, said I,
After so foul a journey death is fair,
      And but a chair.

DISCIPLINE

  Throw away Thy rod,
  Throw away Thy wrath:
    O my God,
  Take the gentle path.

  For my heart's desire
  Unto Thine is bent:
    I aspire
  To a full consent.

  Not a word or look
  I affect to own,
    But by book,
  And Thy book alone.

Though I fail, I weep:
Though I halt in pace,
   Yet I creep
To the throne of grace.

Then let wrath remove;
Love will do the deed:
   For with love
Stony hearts will bleed.

Love is swift of foot;
Love's a man of war
   And can shoot,
And can hit from far.

Who can 'scape his bow?
That which wrought on Thee,
   Brought Thee low,
Needs must work on me.

Throw away Thy rod;
Though man frailties hath,
   Thou art God:
Throw away Thy wrath.

THE FLOWER

How fresh, O Lord, how sweet and clean
Are Thy returns! ev'n as the flowers in spring;
  To which besides their own demean,
The late-pass'd frosts tributes of pleasure bring.
        Grief melts away
        Like snow in May,
  As if there were no such cold thing.

Who would have thought my shrivell'd heart
Could have recover'd greenness?   It was gone
  Quite underground; as flowers depart
To see their mother-root, when they have
    blown;
        Where they together
        All the hard weather,
  Dead to the world, keep house unknown.

These are Thy wonders, Lord of power,
Killing and quick'ning, bringing down to hell
  And up to heaven in an hour;
Making a chiming of a passing-bell.
        We say amiss,
        This or that is:
  Thy word is all, if we could spell.

O that I once pass'd changing were,
Fast in Thy Paradise, where no flower can
    wither!

Many a spring I shoot up fair,
Off'ring at heaven, growing and groaning thither:
      Nor doth my flower
      Want a spring-shower,
My sins and I joining together:

But while I grow in a straight line,
Still upwards bent, as if heav'n were mine own,
  Thy anger comes, and I decline:
What frost to that? what pole is not the zone,
      Where all things burn,
      When Thou dost turn,
And the least frown of Thine is shown?

And now in age I bud again,
After so many deaths I live and write;
  I once more smell the dew and rain
And relish versing: O my only light,
      It cannot be
      That I am he
On whom Thy tempests fell all night.

These are Thy wonders, Lord of love,
To make us see we are but flowers that glide:
  Which when we once can find and prove,
Thou hast a garden for us, where to bide.
      Who would be more,
      Swelling through store,
Forfeit their Paradise by their pride.

THE ELIXIR

    Teach me, my God and King,
      In all things Thee to see,
And what I do in anything,
      To do it as for Thee:

    Not rudely, as a beast,
      To run into an action;
But still to make Thee prepossest,
      And give it his[1] perfection.

    A man that looks on glass,
      On it may stay his eye;
Or if he pleaseth, through it pass,
      And then the heav'n espy.

    All may of Thee partake:
      Nothing can be so mean,
Which with his[1] tincture, *for Thy sake*,
      Will not grow bright and clean.

    A servant with this clause
      Makes drudgery divine:
Who sweeps a room, as for Thy laws,
      Makes that and th' action fine.

    This is the famous stone
      That turneth all to gold;
For that which God doth touch and own
      Cannot for less be told.

[1] Its.

EMPLOYMENT

If as a flower doth spread and die,
  Thou wouldst extend me to some good,
Before I were by frost's extremity
    Nipt in the bud;

The sweetness and the praise were Thine;
  But the extension and the room
Which in Thy garland I should fill were mine
    At Thy great doom.

For as Thou dost impart Thy grace,
  The greater shall our glory be.
The measure of our joys is in this place,
    The stuff with Thee.

Let me not languish then, and spend
  A life as barren to Thy praise,
As is the dust, to which that life doth tend
    But with delays.

All things are busy; only I
  Neither bring honey with the bees,
Nor flowers to make that, nor the husbandry
    To water these.

I am no link of Thy great chain,
  But all my company is a weed.
Lord, place me in Thy concert; give one strain
    To my poor reed.

DIALOGUE

Sweetest Saviour, if my soul
   Were but worth the having,
Quickly should I then control
   Any thought of waving.
But when all my care and pains
Cannot give the name of gains
To Thy wretch so full of stains,
What delight or hope remains?

What, child, is the balance thine,
   Thine the poise and measure?
If I say, Thou shalt be Mine,
   Finger not My treasure.
What the gains in having thee
Do amount to, only He,
Who for man was sold, can see;
That transferr'd th' accounts to Me.

CHURCH MUSIC

Sweetest of sweets, I thank you: when displeasure
   Did through my body wound my mind,
You took me thence, and in your house of pleasure
   A dainty lodging me assign'd.

Now I in you without a body move,
  Rising and falling with your wings:
We both together sweetly live and love,
  Yet say sometimes, *God help poor Kings.*

Comfort, I'll die ; for if you post from me,
  Sure I shall do so, and much more :
But if I travel in your company,
  You know the way to heaven's door.

PRAISE

O SACRED Providence, who from end to end
Strongly and sweetly movest ! shall I write
And not of Thee, through whom my fingers bend
To hold my quill? shall they not do Thee right?

Of all the creatures both in sea and land
Only to man Thou hast made known Thy ways,
And put the pen alone into his hand,
And made him secretary of Thy praise.

Man is the world's high priest : he doth present
The sacrifice for all ; while they below
Unto the service mutter an assent,
Such as springs use that fall, and winds that blow.

He that to praise and laud Thee doth refrain
Doth not refrain unto himself alone,
But robs a thousand who would praise Thee fain,
And doth commit a world of sin in one.

Wherefore, most sacred Spirit, I here present
For me and all my fellows praise to Thee :
And just it is that I should pay the rent,
Because the benefit accrues to me.

Thou art in small things great, nor small in any,
Thy even praise can neither rise, nor fall.
Thou art in all things one, in each thing many :
For Thou art infinite in one and all.

THE BIRD

  The bird that sees a dainty bower
Made in the tree, where she was wont to sit,
  Wonders and sings, but not His power
Who made the arbour ; this exceeds her wit
      But man doth know
    The spring, whence all things flow.

  And yet, as though he knew it not,
His knowledge winks, and lets his humours reign ;
  They make his life a constant blot,
And all the blood of God to run in vain.
      Ah, wretch ! what verse
    Can thy strange ways rehearse ?

THE TEMPER

How should I praise Thee, Lord! how should
    my rhymes
  Gladly engrave Thy love in steel,
  If what my soul doth feel sometimes,
    My soul might ever feel!

Whether I fly with angels, fall with dust,
  Thy hands made both, and I am there:
  Thy power and love, my love and trust
    Make one place everywhere.

REGENERATION

Surely if each one saw another's heart,
    There would be no commèrce,
  No sale or bargain pass: all would disperse
    And live apart.

  Lord, mend or rather make us: one creation
    Will not suffice our turn:
  Except Thou make us daily, we shall spurn
    Our own salvation.

DIVINITY

Love God, and love your neighbour. Watch
  and pray.
    Do as you would be done unto.
O dark instructions; ev'n as dark as day!
    Who can these Gordian knots undo?

                    George Herbert.

FALSE WORLD

FALSE world, thou liest: thou canst not lend
      The least delight:
Thy favours cannot gain a friend,
      They are so slight:
Thy morning pleasures make an end
      To please at night:
Poor are the wants that thou supply'st;
And yet thou vaunt'st, and yet thou vy'st
With heaven; fond earth, thou boast'st; false
   world, thou liest.

Thy babbling tongue tells golden tales
      Of endless treasure:
Thy bounty offers easy sales
      Of lasting pleasure;
Thou ask'st the conscience what she ails,
      And swear'st to ease her:
There's none can want where thou supply'st,
There's none can give where thou deny'st,
Alas! fond world, thou boast'st; false world,
   thou liest.

What well advisèd ear regards
    What earth can say?
Thy words are gold, but thy rewards
    Are painted clay:
Thy cunning can but pack the cards,
    Thou canst not play:
Thy game at weakest, still thou vy'st;
If seen, and then revy'd, deny'st;
Thou art not what thou seem'st; false world,
    thou liest.

Thy tinsel bosom seems a mint
    Of new-coin'd treasure;
A Paradise, that has no stint,
    No change, no measure;
A painted cask, but nothing in't,
    Nor wealth, nor pleasure;
Vain earth! that falsely thus comply'st
With man; vain man, that thou rely'st
On earth; vain man, thou doat'st; vain earth,
    thou liest.

What mean dull souls, in this high measure
    To haberdash
In earth's base wares, whose greatest treasure
    Is dross and trash;
The height of whose enchanting pleasure
    Is but a flash?
Are these the goods that thou supply'st
Us mortals with? are these the high'st?
Can these bring cordial peace? False world,
    thou liest.

THE THRESHING FLOOR

The world's a floor, whose swelling heaps retain
  The mingled wages of the ploughman's toil;
The world's a heap, whose yet unwinnow'd grain
  Is lodged with chaff and buried in her soil;
All things are mix'd, the useful with the vain;
  The good with bad, the noble with the vile;
    The world's an ark, wherein things pure and gross
      Present their lossful gain, and gainful loss,
Where ev'ry pound of gold contains a pound of dross.

This furnish'd ark presents the greedy view
  With all that earth can give, or heav'n can add;
Here lasting joys, here pleasures hourly new,
  And hourly fading, may be wish'd and had:
All points of honour, counterfeit and true,
  Salute thy soul, and wealth both good and bad:
    Here may'st thou open wide the two-leaved door
      Of all thy wishes, to receive that store,
Which being empty most, does overflow the more.

Come then, my soul, approach this royal burse,
  And see what wares our great exchange retains ;
Come, come ; here's that shall make a firm divorce
  Betwixt thy wants and thee, if want complains ;
No need to sit in council with thy purse,
  Here's nothing good shall cost more price than pains :
    But, O my soul, take heed, if thou rely
    Upon thy faithless optics, thou wilt buy
Too blind a bargain : know, fools only trade by th' eye.

The worldly wisdom of the foolish man
  Is like a sieve, that does alone retain
The grosser substance of the worthless bran :
  But thou, my soul, let thy brave thoughts disdain
So coarse a purchase : O be thou a fan
  To purge the chaff, and keep the winnow'd grain ;
    Make clean thy thoughts, and dress thy mix'd desires :
    Thou art heav'n's tasker ; and thy God requires
The purest of thy flow'r, as well as of thy fires.

Let grace conduct thee to the paths of peace,
  And wisdom bless the soul's unblemish'd ways;
No matter, then, how short or long's the lease,
  Whose date determines thy self-number'd days:
No need to care for wealth's or fame's increase,
  Nor Mars his palm, nor high Apollo's bays.
    Lord, if thy gracious bounty please to fill
    The floor of my desires, and teach me skill
To dress and choose the corn, take those the chaff that will.

THE FOIL

'Tis but a foil at best, and that's the most
        Your skill can boast:
My slipp'ry footing fail'd me; and you trip't,
        Just as I slipt:
My wanton weakness did herself betray
        With too much play:
I was too bold: he never yet stood sure,
        That stands secure:
Who ever trusted to his native strength,
        But fell at length?
The title's craz'd, the tenure is not good,
  That claims by th' evidence of flesh and blood.

Boast not thy skill; the righteous man falls oft,
          Yet falls but soft:
There may be dirt to mire him, but no stones
          To crush his bones:
What if he staggers? Nay, but case he be
          Foil'd on his knee?
That very knee will bend to heav'n, and woo
          For mercy too.
The true-bred gamester ups afresh, and then
          Falls to't again;
Whereas the leaden-hearted coward lies,
And yields his conquer'd life, or craven'd dies.

THE LOADSTONE

Like to the arctic needle, that doth guide
    The wand'ring shade by his magnetic pow'r,
And leaves his silken gnomon to decide
    The question of the controverted hour,
First frantics up and down from side to side,
      And restless beats his crystal'd iv'ry case,
      With vain impatience jets from place to place,
And seeks the bosom of his frozen bride;
      At length he slacks his motion, and doth rest
His trembling point at his bright pole's beloved breast.

E'en so my soul, being hurried here and there,
   By ev'ry object that presents delight,
Fain would be settled, but she knows not where ;
   She likes at morning what she loathes at night :
She bows to honour ; then she lends an ear
     To that sweet swan-like voice of dying pleasure
     Then tumbles in the scatter'd heaps of treasure ;
Now flatter'd with false hope ; now foil'd with fear ;
   Thus finding all the world's delight to be
But empty toys, good God, she points alone to Thee.

But hath the virtued steel a power to move ?
   Or can the untouch'd needle point aright ?
Or can my wand'ring thoughts forbear to rove,
   Unguided by the virtue of Thy Sp'rit ?
O hath my leaden soul the art t' improve
     Her wasted talent, and unrais'd, aspire
     In this sad moulting time of her desire ?
Not first belov'd, have I the power to love ?
     I cannot stir, but as Thou please to move me,
Nor can my heart return Thee love, until Thou love me.

The still commandress of the silent night
  Borrows her beams from her bright brother's
    eye ;
His fair aspect fills her sharp horns with light,
  If he withdraw, her flames are quench'd and
    die :
E'en so the beams of Thy enlight'ning Sp'rit,
  Infus'd and shot into my dark desire,
  Inflame my thoughts, and fill my soul with
    fire,
That I am ravish'd with a new delight ;
  But if Thou shroud Thy face, my glory
    fades,
And I remain a nothing, all composed of
    shades.

Eternal God ! O Thou that only art
  The sacred fountain of eternal light,
And blessed loadstone of my better part,
  O Thou, my heart's desire, my soul's delight !
Reflect upon my soul, and touch my heart,
    And then my heart shall prize no good
      above Thee
    And then my soul shall know Thee ; know-
      ing, love Thee ;
And then my trembling thoughts shall never
    start
    From Thy commands, or swerve the least
      degree,
Or once presume to move, but as they move in
    Thee.

THE BIRDCAGE

My soul is like a bird, my flesh the cage,
Wherein she wears her weary pilgrimage
Of hours, as few as evil, daily fed
With sacred wine and sacramental bread;
The keys that lock her in and let her out,
Are birth and death; 'twixt both she hops about
From perch to perch, from sense to reason;
    then
From higher reason down to sense again:
From sense she climbs to faith; where for a
    season
She sits and sings; then down again to reason:
From reason back to faith, and straight from
    thence
She rudely flutters to the perch of sense:
From sense to hope; then hops from hope to
    doubt,
From doubt to dull despair; there seeks about
For desp'rate freedom, and at ev'ry grate
She wildly thrusts, and begs the untimely date
Of th' unexpired thraldom, to release
The afflicted captive, that can find no peace.
Thus am I coop'd; within this fleshly cage
I wear my youth, and waste my weary age;
Spending that breath, which was ordain'd to
    chant
Heav'n's praises forth, in sighs and sad com-
    plaint.

Francis Quarles.

THE CHRISTIAN STOIC

The man of life upright,
   Whose guiltless heart is free
From all dishonest deeds,
   Or thought of vanity ;

The man whose silent days
   In harmless joys are spent,
Whom hopes cannot delude
   Nor sorrow discontent :

That man needs neither towers
   Nor armour for defence,
Nor secret vaults to fly
   From thunder's violence :

He only can behold
   With unaffrighted eyes
The horrors of the deep
   And terrors of the skies.

Thus scorning all the cares
   That fate or fortune brings,
He makes the heaven his book,
   His wisdom heavenly things,

>   Good thoughts his only friends,
>   His wealth a well-spent age,
>   The earth his sober inn
>   And quiet pilgrimage.

SONG

AUTHOR of life, revive my dying sprite!
Redeem it from the snares of all-confounding
    night!
    Lord, light me to Thy blessed way!
For blind with worldly vain desires I wander
    as astray.
Sun and moon, stars and under-lights I see;
But all their glorious beams are mist and dark-
    ness, being compared to Thee.

Fountain of health, my soul's deep wounds re-
    cure!
Sweet showers of pity rain, wash my unclean-
    ness pure!
    One drop of Thy desired grace
The faint and fading heart can raise, and in
    joy's bosom place.
Sin and death, hell and tempting fiends may
    rage,
But God His own will guard, and their sharp
    pains and grief in time assuage.

SONG

Never weather-beaten sail more willing bent
    to shore,
Never tired pilgrim's limbs affected slumber
    more,
Than my wearied sprite now longs to fly out of
    my troubled breast.
O come quickly, sweetest Lord, and take my
    soul to rest!

Ever blooming are the joys of heaven's high
    Paradise,
Cold age deafs not there our ears nor vapour
    dims our eyes:
Glory there the sun outshines; whose beams
    the blessèd only see.
O come quickly, glorious Lord, and raise my
    sprite to Thee!

Thomas Campion.

DIALOGUE

Soul. Ay me, poor soul, whom bound in sinful chains
This wretched body keeps against my will!
Body. Ay me, poor body, whom for all my pains
This froward soul causeless condemneth still.
Soul. Causeless? whenas thou striv'st to sin each day!
Body. Causeless! whenas I strive thee to obey!

Soul. Thou art the means by which I fall to sin.
Body. Thou art the cause that set'st this means a-work.
Soul. No part of thee that hath not faulty been.
Body. I show the poison that in thee doth lurk.
Soul. I shall be pure whenso I part from thee.
Body. So were I now but that thou stainest me.

Though late, my heart, yet turn at last,
And shape thy course another way ;
'Tis better lose thy labour past
Than follow on to sure decay :
 What though thou long have strayed awry?
 In hope of grace for mercy cry.

Though weight of sin doth press thee down
And keep thee grovelling on the ground ;
Though black Despair, with angry frown,
Thy wit and judgment quite confound ;
 Though time and wit have been misspent,
 Yet grace is left if thou repent.

Weep then, my heart, weep still and still,
Nay, melt to floods of flowing tears ;
Send out such shrieks as heaven may fill
And pierce thine angry Judge's ears,
 And let thy soul, that harbours sin,
 Bleed streams of blood to drown it in.

Then shall thine angry Judge's face
To cheerful looks itself apply ;
Then shall thy soul be filled with grace,
And fear of death constrained to fly.
 Even so, my God ! oh when ? how long ?
 I would, but sin is too, too strong.

I strive to rise, sin keeps me down ;
I fly from sin, sin follows me.
My will doth reach at glory's crown ;
Weak is my strength, it will not be.
    See how my fainting soul doth pant ;
    Oh, let Thy strength supply my want.

A. W.

SOUL AND BODY

Poor soul! the centre of my sinful earth,
Fool'd by[1] these rebel powers that thee array,
Why dost thou pine within and suffer dearth,
Painting thy outward walls so costly gay?

Why so large cost, having so short a lease,
Dost thou upon thy fading mansion spend?
Shall worms, inheritors of this excess,
Eat up thy charge? is this thy body's end?

Then, soul, live thou upon thy servant's loss,
And let that pine to aggravate thy store;
Buy terms divine in selling hours of dross;
Within be fed, without be rich no more;

So shalt thou feed on Death, that feeds on men,
And Death once dead, there's no more dying
    then.

W. Shakespeare.

[1] Malone: "pressed by," Dowden. The first two words are lost, and have been variously supplied.

URBS BEATA HIERUSALEM

Hierusalem, my happy home,
  When shall I come to thee?
When shall my sorrows have an end?
  Thy joys when shall I see?

O happy harbour of the saints,
  O sweet and pleasant soil,
In thee no sorrow may be found,
  No grief, no care, no toil!

No dampish mist is seen in thee,
  No cold nor darksome night;
There every soul shines as the sun;
  There God Himself gives light.

There lust and lucre cannot dwell,
  There envy bears no sway;
There is no hunger, heat, nor cold,
  But pleasure every way.

Hierusalem! Hierusalem!
  God grant I once[1] may see
Thy endless joys, and of the same
  Partaker aye to be.

[1] At last.

Thy walls are made of precious stones,
   Thy bulwarks diamonds square,
Thy gates are of right orient pearl,
   Exceeding rich and rare.

Thy turrets and thy pinnacles
   With carbuncles do shine,
Thy very streets are paved with gold
   Surpassing clear and fine.

Thy houses are of ivory,
   Thy windows crystal clear,
Thy tiles are made of beaten gold,—
   O God, that I were there!

Ah, my sweet home, Hierusalem,
   Would God I were in thee!
Would God my woes were at an end,
   Thy joys that I might see!

We that are here in banishment
   Continually do moan,
We sigh and sob, we weep and wail,
   Perpetually we groan.

Our sweet is mixed with bitter gall,
   Our pleasure is but pain;
Our joys scarce last the looking on,
   Our sorrows still remain.

But there they live in such delight,
  Such pleasure and such play,
As that to them a thousand years
  Doth seem as yesterday.

Thy gardens and thy gallant walks
  Continually are green;
There grow such sweet and pleasant flowers
  As nowhere else are seen.

Quite through the streets with silver sound
  The flood of life doth flow,
Upon whose banks on every side
  The wood of life doth grow.

There trees for evermore bear fruit,
  And evermore do spring;
There evermore the angels sit,
  And evermore do sing.

There David stands, with harp in hands
  As master of the choir,
Ten thousand times that man were blest
  That might this music hear.

Our Lady sings Magnificat
  With tones surpassing sweet,
And all the virgins bear their part,
  Sitting about her feet.

There Magdalene hath left her moan,
    And cheerfully doth sing
With blessed saints, whose harmony
    In every street doth ring.

Hierusalem, my happy home,
    Would God I were in thee!
Would God my woes were at an end,
    Thy joys that I might see! Amen.

F. B. P.

THE INVITATION

Lord, what unvalued pleasures crown'd
    The days of old ;
When Thou wert so familiar found,
    Those days were gold ;

When Abram wished, Thou could'st afford
    With him to feast ;
When Lot but said, "Turn in, my Lord,"
    Thou wert his guest.

But ah ! this heart of mine doth pant
    And beat for Thee ;
Yet Thou art strange, and will not grant
    Thyself to me !

What, shall thy people be so dear
    To Thee no more ?
Or is not heaven to earth as near
    As heretofore ?

The famished raven's hoarser cry
    Finds out Thine ear ;
My soul is famished and I die
    Unless Thou hear.

THE HEART'S CHAMBERS

If I could shut the gate against my thoughts
   And keep out sorrow from this room within,
Or memory could cancel all the notes
   Of my misdeeds, and I unthink my sin :
How free, how clear, how clean my soul should lie,
Discharged of such a loathsome company !

Or were there other rooms without my heart
   That did not to my conscience join so near,
Where I might lodge the thoughts of sin apart
   That I might not their clam'rous crying hear ;
What peace, what joy, what ease should I possess,
Freed from their horrors that my soul oppress !
But, O my Saviour, who my refuge art,
   Let Thy dear mercies stand 'twixt them and me,
And be the wall to separate my heart,
   So that I may at length repose me free ;
That peace, and joy, and rest may be within,
And I remain divided from my sin.

CONFESSION

Let not the sluggish sleep
   Close up thy waking eye,
Until with judgment deep
   Thy daily deeds thou try :

He that one sin in conscience keeps
    When he to quiet goes,
More vent'rous is than he that sleeps
    With twenty mortal foes.

A ROYAL GUEST

YET if his majesty our sovereign lord
Should of his own accord
Friendly himself invite,
And say "I'll be your guest to-morrow night,"
How should we stir ourselves, call and command
All hands to work! "Let no man idle stand.
Set me fine Spanish tables in the hall,
See they be fitted all;
Let there be room to eat,
And order taken that there want no meat.
See every sconce and candlestick made bright,
That without tapers they may give a light.
Look to the presence: are the carpets spread,
The dais o'er the head,
The cushions in the chairs,
And all the candles lighted on the stairs?
Perfume the chambers, and in any case
Let each man give attendance in his place."
Thus if the king were coming would we do,
And 'twere good reason too;
For 'tis a duteous thing
To show all honour to an earthly king,

And after all our travail and our cost,
So he be pleased, to think no labour lost.
But at the coming of the King of Heaven
All's set at six and seven :
We wallow in our sin,
Christ cannot find a chamber in the inn.
We entertain Him always like a stranger,
And as at first still lodge Him in the manger.

Anon.

A SONG OF DIVINE LOVE

Lord ! when the sense of Thy sweet grace
Sends up my soul to seek Thy face,
Thy blessed eyes breed such desire,
I die in love's delicious fire.
O love ! I am thy sacrifice ;
Be still triumphant, blessed eyes.
Still shine on me, fair sun ; that I
Still may behold, though still I die.

Though still I die, I live again,
Still longing so to be still slain,
So gainful is such loss of breath,
I die even in desire of death.
Still live in me this longing strife
Of living death and dying life,
For, while Thou sweetly slayest me,
Dead to myself, I live in Thee.

EASTER DAY

Rise, Heir of fresh eternity
    From Thy virgin tomb ;
Rise, mighty Man of wonders, and Thy world
    with thee ;
    Thy tomb the universal east,
        Nature's new womb,
Thy tomb fair immortality's perfumed nest.

Of all the glories make noon gay,
    This is the morn ;
This rock buds forth the fountain of the
    streams of day ;
    In joy's white annals lives this hour
        When life was born,
No cloud scowl on his radiant lids, no tempest
    low'r.

Life, by this Light's nativity,
    All creatures have ;
Death only by this day's just doom is forced to
    die :
    Nor is Death forced ; for may he lie
        Throned in Thy grave,
Death will on this condition be content to die.

    Christ when He died
    Deceived the cross,
    And on Death's side
    Threw all the loss.
The captive world awaked and found
The prisoners loose, the jailor bound.

    O dear and sweet dispute
'Twixt Death's and Love's far different fruit,
    Different as far
As antidotes and poisons are :

By the first fatal tree
Both Life and Liberty
    Were sold and slain ;
By this they both look up and live again.

O strange mysterious strife
Of open death and hidden life !
When on the cross my King did bleed,
Life seem'd to die, Death died indeed.

TO THE NAME ABOVE EVERY NAME, THE NAME OF JESUS

A HYMN

I SING the Name which none can say,
But touch'd with an interior ray ;
The Name of our new peace, our good,
Our bliss, and supernatural blood.
The Name of all our lives and loves.
Hearken and help, ye holy doves,
The high-born brood of day, the bright
Candidates of blissful light,
The heirs-elect of love, whose names belong
Unto the everlasting life of song ;
All ye wise souls, who in the wealthy breast
Of this unbounded Name build your warm nest ;
Awake my glory, soul (if such thou be
And that fair word at all refer to thee),

                Awake and sing
                And be all wing,
Bring hither thy whole self, and let me see
What of thy parent Heaven yet speaks in
    thee;
                O thou art poor
                Of noble powers, I see,
And full of nothing else but empty me,
Narrow; and low, and infinitely less
Than this great morning's mighty business.
                One little word or two
                (Alas) will never do;
                We must have store,
Go, soul, out of thyself, and seek for more;
                Go and request
Great Nature for the key of her huge chest
Of heav'ns, the self-involving set of spheres,
Which dull mortality more feels than hears;
                Then rouse the nest
Of nimble art, and traverse round
The airy shop of soul-appeasing sound,
        And beat a summons in the same
                All Sovereign Name,
        To warn each several kind
        And shape of sweetness, be they such
                As sigh with supple wind,
                Or answer artful touch,
        That they convene and come away,
To wait at the love-crowned doors of this
    illustrious day.

Shall we dare this, my soul? we'll do't and
  bring
No other note for't but the Name we sing.
    Wake, lute and harp,
    And every sweet-lipt thing
    That talks with tuneful string,
Start into life: and leap with me
Into a habit fit of self-tuned harmony;
    Nor must you think it much
    T' obey my bolder touch.
I have authority in Love's name to take you,
And to the work of love this morning wake you;
    Wake in the Name
Of Him who never sleeps, all things that are,
    Or, what's the same,
    Are musical,
    Answer my call
    And come along,
Help me to meditate mine immortal song.
Come, ye soft ministers of sweet sad mirth,
Bring all your household stuff of heav'n on
  earth;
  O you my soul's most certain wings,
  Complaining pipes, and prattling strings,
    Bring all the store
Of sweets you have, and murmur that you
  have no more.
Come, lovely Name, appear forth from the bright
  Regions of peaceful light,
  Look from Thine own illustrious home,
  Fair King of Names, and come,

Leave all Thy native glories in their gorgeous
    nest,
And give Thyself awhile the gracious guest
    Of humble souls, that seek to find
        The hidden sweets
        Which man's heart meets,
    When Thou art master of the mind.
    Come, lovely Name, life of our hope!
    Lo, we hold our hearts wide ope!
    Unlock Thy cabinet of day,
    Dearest sweet, and come away.
        Lo, how the thirsty lands
Gasp for Thy golden showers, with long-
    stretched hands!

        Lo, how the labouring earth,
            That hopes to be
            All heavens by Thee,
            Leaps at Thy birth.
Come, royal Name, and pay th' expense
Of all Thy precious patience.
        O! come away,
        And kill the death of this delay.
O! see so many worlds of barren years
Melted, and measured out in seas of tears;
O! see, the weary lids of wakeful hope
(Love's eastern windows) all wide ope
        With curtains drawn,
To catch the daybreak of Thy dawn;
O! dawn at last, long-look'd for day,
Take thine own wings and come away.

 Sweet Name, in Thy each syllable
A thousand blest Arabias dwell,
A thousand hills of frankincense ;
Mountains of myrrh, and beds of spices,
And ten thousand paradises
 The soul that tastes Thee takes from thence.
How many unknown worlds there are
 Of comforts which Thou hast in keeping !
How many thousand mercies there,
 In Pity's lost lap, lie a-sleeping !
Happy he who has the art
   To awake them,
   And to take them
Home and lodge them in his heart.
O that it were as it was wont to be !
When Thy old friends of fire, all full of Thee,
Fought against frowns with smiles, gave
 glorious chase
To persecutions, and against the face
Of death and fiercest dangers, durst with brave
And sober pace, march on to meet a grave.
On their bold breasts about the world they bare
 Thee,
And to the teeth of hell stood up to teach Thee :
In centre of their inmost souls they wore Thee
Where racks and torments strived in vain to
 reach Thee.
   Little, alas ! thought they
  Who tore the fair breasts of thy friends,
   Their fury but made way
For Thee; and served therein Thy glorious ends.

What did their weapons but set wide the doors
  For Thee? Fair purple doors of Love's
    devising;
The ruby windows which enriched the east
    Of Thy so oft-repeated rising.
Each wound of theirs was Thy new morning;
And re-enthroned Thee in Thy rosy nest,
  With blush of Thine own blood Thy day
    adorning.
It was the wit of love o'erflowed the bounds
Of wrath, and made Thee way through all those
    wounds.

THE DEAR BARGAIN

LORD! what is man? why should he cost you
So dear? what had his ruin lost you?
Lord! what is man, that Thou hast over-
  bought
    So much a thing of nought?
Love is too kind, I see, and can
Make but a simple merchant man;
'Twas for such sorry merchandise,
Bold painters have put out his eyes.
Alas! sweet Lord, what wer't to Thee,
If there were no such worms as we?
  Heaven ne'er the less still heav'n would be
    Should mankind dwell
    In the deep hell,
What have his woes to do with Thee?

Let him go weep
O'er his own wounds,
Seraphims will not sleep,
Nor spheres let fall their faithful rounds:
Still would the youthful spirits sing,
And still the spacious palace ring:
Still would those beauteous ministers of light
Burn all as bright,
And bow their flaming heads before Thee,
Still thrones and dominations would adore Thee,
Still would those wakeful sons of fire
Keep warm Thy praise
Both nights and days,
And teach Thy loved name to their noble lyre.
Let froward dust then do its kind,
And give itself for sport to the proud wind;
Why should a piece of peevish clay plead shares
In the eternity of Thy old cares?
Why should'st Thou bow Thy awful breast to see
What mine own madnesses have done with me?
Should not the king still keep his throne,
Because some desperate fool's undone?
Or will the world's illustrious eyes
Weep for every worm that dies?
Will the gallant sun
E'er the less glorious run?
Will he hang down his golden head,
Or e'er the sooner seek his western bed,
Because some foolish fly
Grows wanton, and will die?

If I was lost in misery
What was it to Thy heav'n and Thee?
What was it to the precious blood,
If my foul heart call'd for a flood?
What if my faithless soul and I
   Would needs fall in
   With guilt and sin?
 What did the Lamb that He should die?
 What did the Lamb that He should need,
 When the wolf sins, Himself to bleed?
   If my base lust
Bargain'd with death, and well beseeming dust;
   Why should the white
   Lamb's bosom write
   The purple name
   Of my sin's shame?
Why should His unstain'd breast make good
My blushes with His own heart-blood?

O my Saviour, make me see,
How dearly Thou hast paid for me,
That, lost again, my life may prove,
As then in death, so now in love.

S. MARY MAGDALENE

 Not in the evening's eyes
 When they red with weeping are
  For the sun that dies
 Sits sorrow with a face so fair:
Nowhere but here did ever meet
Sweetness so sad, sadness so sweet

When Sorrow would be seen
In her brightest majesty
   (For she is a queen),
Then is she dress'd by none but Thee.
Then, and only then, she wears
Her proudest pearls, I mean Thy tears.

The dew no more will weep,
The primrose's pale cheek to deck;
   The dew no more will sleep,
Nuzzled in the lily's neck:
Much rather would it be Thy tear,
And leave them both to tremble here.

A HYMN TO S. TERESA

Love, thou art absolute, sole lord
Of life and death. To prove the word,
We'll now appeal to none of all
Those thy old soldiers, great and tall,
Ripe men of martyrdom, that could reach
   down,
With strong arms their triumphant crown:
Such as could with lusty breath
Speak loud into the face of death
Their great Lord's glorious name; to none
Of those whose spacious bosoms spread a
   throne

For love at large to fill: spare blood and
    sweat;
We'll see him take a private seat,
Making his mansion in the mild
And milky soul of a soft child.
Scarce hath she learn'd to lisp the name
Of martyr; yet she thinks it shame
Life should so long play with that breath,
Which spent can buy so brave a **death**.
She never undertook to know
What death with love should have to do;
Nor hath she e'er yet understood,
Why to show love, she should shed blood;
Yet though she cannot tell you why,
She can love, and she can die.
Scarce hath she blood enough to make
A guilty sword blush for her sake;
Yet hath she a heart dare hope to prove,
How much less strong is death than love.
   Since 'tis not to be had at home,
She'll travel for a martyrdom.
No home for her, confesses she,
But where she may a martyr be.
She'll to the Moors, and trade with them
For this unvalued diadem;
She'll offer them her dearest breath,
With Christ's name in't, in change for death.
She'll bargain with them, and will give
Them God, and teach them how to live
In Him; or if they this deny,
For Him she'll teach them how to die.

So shall she leave amongst them sown
Her Lord's blood, or at least her own.
Farewell, then, all the world! adieu,
Teresa is no more for you:
Farewell all pleasures, sports, and joys,
(Never till now esteemed toys):
Farewell whatever dear may be,
Mother's arms, or father's knee:
Farewell house, and farewell home,
She's for the Moors and martyrdom.

Sweet, not so fast! lo, thy fair spouse,
Whom thou seek'st with so swift vows,
Calls thee back, and bids thee come,
T' embrace a milder martyrdom.
O how oft shalt thou complain
Of a sweet and subtle pain!
Of intolerable joys!
Of a death in which who dies
Loves his death, and dies again,
And would for ever so be slain!
And lives, and dies; and knows not why
To live, but that he thus may never leave to die
How kindly will thy gentle heart
Kiss the sweetly-killing dart?
And close in thine embraces keep
Those delicious wounds that weep
Balsam to heal themselves with. Thus
When these thy deaths so numerous,
Shall all at last die into one,
And melt thy soul's sweet mansion;

Like a soft lump of incense hasted
By too hot a fire, and wasted
Into perfuming clouds, so fast
Shall thou exhale to heav'n at last,
In a resolving sigh, and then,
O what?—ask not the tongues of men.
Angels cannot tell. Suffice,
Thyself shall feel thine own full joys,
And hold them fast for ever. There,
So soon as thou shall first appear,
The moon of maiden stars, thy white
Mistress attended by such bright
Souls as thy shining self, shall come,
And in her first ranks make thee room,
Where 'mongst her snowy family,
Immortal welcomes wait for thee.
O what delight when she shall stand
And teach thy lips heav'n with her hand,
On which thou now may'st to thy wishes,
Heap up thy consecrated kisses!
What joys shall seize thy soul, when she,
Bending her blessed eyes on thee
(Those second smiles of heav'n), shall dart
Her mild rays through thy melting heart!
Angels, thy old friends, there shall greet thee,
Glad at their own home now to meet thee.
All thy good works which went before,
And waited for thee at the door,
Shall own thee there, and all in one
Weave a constellation

Of crowns, with which the King thy spouse,
Shall build up thy triumphant brows;
All thy old woes shall now smile on thee,
And thy pains sit bright upon thee.
All thy sorrows here shall shine,
And all thy suff'rings be divine;
Tears shall take comfort and turn gems,
And wrongs repent to diadems.
Ev'n thy deaths shall live, and new
Dress the soul that erst they slew.
Thy wounds shall blush to such bright scars,
As keep account of the Lamb's wars.
Those rare works where thou shalt leave writ
Love's noble history, with wit
Taught thee by none but Him, while here
They feed our souls, shall clothe thine there.
Each heavenly word by whose hid flame
Our hard hearts shall strike fire, the same
Shall flourish on thy brows, and be
Both fire to us, and flame to thee;
Whose light shall live bright, in thy face
By glory, in our hearts by grace.
Thou shalt look round about, and see
Thousands of crown'd souls throng to be
Themselves thy crown; sons of thy vows,
The virgin-births, with which thy sovereign
    spouse
Made fruitful thy fair soul. Go now,
And with them all about thee, bow
To Him; put on (He'll say) put on
(My rosy love) that thy rich zone,

Sparkling with the sacred flames
Of thousand souls whose happy names
Heav'n keeps upon thy score (thy bright
Life brought them first to kiss the light,
That kindled then to stars) and so
Thou with the Lamb, thy Lord, shalt go,
And whereso'er He sets His white
Steps, walk with Him those ways of light;
Which who in death would live to see,
Must learn in life to die like thee.

UPON THE BOOK AND PICTURE OF THE SERAPHICAL SAINT TERESA

FROM THE "FLAMING HEART"

O THOU undaunted daughter of desires!
By all thy dower of lights and fires;
By all the eagle in thee, all the dove;
By all thy lives and deaths of love;
By thy large draughts of intellectual day,
And by thy thirsts of love more large than they;
By all thy brim-filled bowls of fierce desire,
By thy last morning's draught of liquid fire;
By the full kingdom of that final kiss
That seized thy parting soul, and sealed thee His;
By all the heav'n thou hast in Him
(Fair sister of the seraphim!),
By all of Him we have in thee,
Leave nothing of myself in me.
Let me so read thy life, that I
Unto all life of mine may die. *R. Crashaw.*

LIFE AND DEATH

FRAIL Life! in which, through mists of human breath
We grope for truth, and make our progress slow,
Because by passion blinded; till, by death
Our passions ending, we begin to know.

O reverend Death! whose looks can soon advise
E'en scornful youth, whilst priests their doctrine waste;
Yet mocks us too; for he does make us wise,
When by his coming our affairs are past.

O harmless Death! whom still the valiant brave,
The wise expect, the sorrowful invite,
And all the good embrace, who know the grave
A short dark passage to eternal light.

Sir W. Davenant.

NOX NOCTI INDICAT SCIENTIAM

When I survey the bright
  Celestial sphere,
So rich with jewels hung, that Night
Doth like an Ethiop bride appear,

  My soul her wings doth spread
    And heavenward flies,
  The Almighty's mysteries to read
  In the large volumes of the skies.

  For the bright firmament
    Shoots forth no flame
  So silent, but is eloquent
  In speaking the Creator's name.

  No unregarded star
    Contracts its light
  Into so small a character,
  Removed far from our human sight,

  But if we steadfast look,
    We shall discern
  In it, as in some holy book,
  How man may heavenly knowledge learn.

It tells the conqueror
    That far-stretch'd power,
Which his proud dangers traffic for,
Is but the triumph of an hour.

That from the farthest north
    Some nation may,
Yet undiscover'd, issue forth,
And o'er his new-got conquest sway;

Some nation yet shut in
    With hills of ice
May be let out to scourge his sin,
Till they shall equal him in vice.

And then they likewise shall
    Their ruin have;
For as yourselves your empires fall,
And every kingdom hath a grave.

Thus those celestial fires,
    Though seeming mute,
The fallacy of our desires
And all the pride of life confute.

For they have watch'd since first
    The world had birth;
And found sin in itself accurst,
And nothing permanent on earth.
                    W. Habington.

AN EVENING PRAYER

Thou whose nature cannot sleep,
On my temples sentry keep;
Guard me 'gainst those watchful foes,
Whose eyes are open whilst mine close;
Let no dreams my head infest,
But such as Jacob's temples blest.
While I do rest, my soul advance;
Make me to sleep a holy trance,
That I may, my rest being wrought,
Awake into some holy thought;
And with as active vigour run
My course, as doth the nimble sun.
Sleep is a death. Oh, make me try
By sleeping, what it is to die!
And as gently lay my head
On my grave, as now my bed.
Howe'er I rest, great God, let me
Awake again at last with Thee!
And thus assured, behold I lie
Securely, or to wake or die.

Sir Thomas Browne.

MORNING HYMN

These are Thy glorious works, Parent of good,
Almighty, Thine this universal frame,
Thus wondrous fair; Thyself how wondrous
   then!
Unspeakable, who sitt'st above these heavens
To us invisible, or dimly seen
In these Thy lowest works; yet these declare
Thy goodness beyond thought, and power
   divine.
Speak, ye who best can tell, ye sons of light,
Angels; for ye behold Him, and with songs
And choral symphonies, day without night,
Circle His throne rejoicing; ye in Heaven.
On Earth join, all ye creatures, to extol
Him first, Him last, Him midst, and without
   end.
Fairest of stars, last in the train of night,
If better thou belong not to the dawn,
Sure pledge of day, that crown'st the smiling
   morn
With thy bright circlet, praise Him in thy
   sphere,
While day arises, that sweet hour of prime.
Thou Sun, of this great world both eye and
   soul,

Acknowledge Him thy greater; sound His praise
In thy eternal course, both when thou climb'st
And when high noon hast gained, and when thou fall'st.
Moon, that now meet'st the orient sun, now fli'st
With the fixed Stars, fixed in their orb that flies;
And ye, five other wandering Fires, that move
In mystic dance not without song, resound
His praise, who out of darkness called up light.
Air, and ye Elements, the eldest birth
Of Nature's womb, that in quaternion run
Perpetual circle, multiform, and mix
And nourish all things, let your ceaseless change
Vary to our great Maker still new praise.
Ye mists and Exhalations, that now rise
From hill or steaming lake, dusky or grey,
Till the sun paint your fleecy skirts with gold,
In honour to the world's great Author rise;
Whether to deck with clouds the uncoloured sky,
Or wet the thirsty earth with falling showers,
Rising or falling still advance His praise.
His praise, ye Winds, that from four quarters blow,
Breathe soft or loud; and wave your tops, ye Pines,
With every plant, in sign of worship wave.
Fountains, and ye that warble, as ye flow,
Melodious murmurs, warbling tune His praise.
Join voices, all ye living Souls. Ye Birds,

That singing up to heaven-gate ascend,
Bear on your wings and in your notes His
    praise.
Ye that in waters glide, and ye that walk
The earth, and stately tread, or lowly creep;
Witness if I be silent, morn or even,
To hill or valley, fountain, or fresh shade,
Made vocal by my song, and taught His praise.
Hail, universal Lord, be bounteous still
To give us only good; and if the night
Have gathered aught of evil, or concealed,
Disperse it, as now light dispels the dark!

THE SPACIOUS FIRMAMENT

AND for the heaven's wide circuit, let it speak
The Maker's high magnificence, who built
So spacious, and His line stretched out so far,
That man may know he dwells not in his own:
An edifice too large for him to fill,
Lodged in a small partition, and the rest
Ordained for uses to his Lord best known.
Nor think, though men were none,
That heaven would want spectators, God want
    praise;
Millions of spiritual creatures walk the earth
Unseen, both when we wake and when we
    sleep;
All these with ceaseless praise His works behold
Both day and night.

UPON THE CIRCUMCISION

Ye flaming Powers, and wingèd warriors bright,
That erst with music and triumphant song,
First heard by happy watchful shepherds' ear,
So sweetly sung your joy the clouds along
Through the soft silence of the listening night,
Now mourn; and if, sad share with us to bear,
Your fiery essence can distil no tear,
Burn in your sighs, and borrow
Seas wept from our deep sorrow;
He who with all heaven's heraldry whilere
Entered the world, now bleeds to give us ease.
Alas, how soon our sin
    Sore doth begin
    His infancy to seize!
Oh, more exceeding love, or law more just?
Just law indeed, but more exceeding love!
For we by rightful doom remediless
Were lost in death, till He that dwelt above
High throned in secret bliss, for us frail dust
Emptied His glory, even to nakedness;
And that great cov'nant which we still transgress
Entirely satisfied,
And the full wrath beside
Of vengeful justice bore for our excess,
And seals obedience first with wounding smart
This day; but oh, ere long
Huge pangs and strong
    Will pierce more near His heart!

GOD'S PROVIDENCE

Many are the sayings of the wise,
In ancient and in modern books enrolled,
Extolling patience as the truest fortitude ;
And to the bearing well of all calamities,
All chances incident to man's frail life,
Consolatories writ
With studied argument, and much persuasion
    sought,
Lenient of grief and anxious thought ;
But with the afflicted in his pangs their sound
Little prevails, or rather seems a tune
Harsh, and of dissonant mood from his com-
    plaint,
Unless he feel within
Some source of consolation from above,
Secret refreshings that repair his strength,
And fainting spirits uphold.

   God of our fathers ! what is man
That Thou towards him with hand so various,
Or might I say contrarious,
Temperest Thy providence through his short
    course,
Not evenly, as Thou rul'st
The angelic orders, and inferior creatures mute,
Irrational and brute ?
Nor do I name of men the common rout,
That, wandering loose about,

Grow up and perish, as the summer fly,
Heads without name, no more rememberèd;
But such as Thou hast solemnly elected,
With gifts and graces eminently adorned,
To some great work, Thy glory,
And people's safety, which in part they effect;
Yet toward these thus dignified, Thou oft
Amidst their highth of noon,
Changest Thy countenance and Thy hand, with
    no regard
Of highest favours past
From Thee on them, or them to Thee of service.

  Not only dost degrade them, or remit
To life obscured, which were a fair dismission,
But throw'st them lower than Thou didst exalt
    them high;
Unseemly falls in human eye,
Too grievous for the trespass or omission;
Oft leavest them to the hostile sword
Of heathen and profane, their carcases
To dogs and fowls a prey, or else captived;
Or to the unjust tribunals, under change of times,
And condemnation of th' ingrateful multitude.
If these they 'scape, perhaps in poverty
With sickness and disease thou bow'st them
    down,
Painful diseases and deformed,
In crude old age;
Though not disordinate, yet causeless suffering,
The punishment of dissolute days; in fine,

Just or unjust alike seem miserable ;
For oft alike both come to evil end.

   Just are the ways of God,
And justifiable to men,
Unless there be who think not God at all.
If any be, they walk obscure ;
For of such doctrine never was there school,
But the heart of the fool,
And no man therein doctor but himself.

All is best, though we oft doubt,
What the unsearchable dispose
Of highest wisdom brings about,
And ever best found in the close.

ON HIS BLINDNESS

WHEN I consider how my light is spent
  Ere half my days, in this dark world and wide,
  And that one talent, which is death to hide,
Lodged with me useless,—though my soul more bent

To serve therewith my Maker, and present
  My true account, lest He, returning, chide,—
  " Doth God exact day-labour, light denied ? "
I fondly ask. But Patience, to prevent

That murmur, soon replies, "God doth not need
  Either man's work or His own gifts; who best
    Bear His mild yoke, they serve Him best: His state
Is kingly; thousands at His bidding speed,
  And post o'er land and ocean without rest;
    They also serve who only stand and wait."

AT A SOLEMN MUSIC

Blest pair of Sirens, pledges of Heaven's joy,
Sphere-born harmonious sisters, Voice and Verse,
Wed your divine sounds, and mix'd power employ
Dead things with inbreathed sense able to pierce;
And to our high-raised fantasy present
That undisturbed song of pure concent,
Aye sung before the sapphire-colour'd throne
To Him that sits thereon,
With saintly shout and solemn jubilee;
Where the bright Seraphim, in burning row,
Their loud uplifted angel trumpets blow;
And the Cherubic host, in thousand quires,
Touch their immortal harps of golden wires,
With those just Spirits that wear victorious palms,
Hymns devout and holy psalms
Singing everlastingly:

That we on earth, with undiscording voice,
May rightly answer that melodious noise;
As once we did, till disproportion'd sin
Jarr'd against nature's chime, and with harsh din
Broke the fair musick that all creatures made
To their great Lord, whose love their motion sway'd
In perfect diapason, whilst they stood
In first obedience and their state of good.
O may we soon again renew that song,
And keep in tune with heaven, till God ere long
To His celestial concert us unite,
To live with Him, and sing in endless morn of light!

ON TIME

TO BE SET ON A CLOCK-CASE

FLY, envious Time, till thou run out thy race;
Call on the lazy leaden-stepping hours,
Whose speed is but the heavy plummet's pace;
And glut thyself with what thy womb devours,
Which is no more than what is false and vain,
And merely human dross;
So little is our loss,
So little is thy gain!
For when as each thing bad thou hast entomb'd,
And last of all thy greedy self consumed,

Then long Eternity shall greet our bliss
With an individual kiss ;
And Joy shall overtake us as a flood,
When everything that is sincerely good
And perfectly divine,
With Truth, and Peace, and Love, shall ever shine
About the supreme throne
Of Him, to whose happy-making sight alone
When once our heavenly-guided soul shall climb ;
Then, all this earthy grossness quit,
Attired with stars we shall for ever sit
Triumphing over Death, and Chance, and thee, O Time.

John Milton.

HYMN FOR ADVENT

    Lord, come away;
    Why dost Thou stay?
Thy road is ready, and Thy paths made straight
With longing expectation wait
The consecration of Thy beauteous feet.
Ride on triumphantly : behold we lay
Our lusts and proud wills in Thy way.
Hosannah ! welcome to our hearts : Lord, here
Thou hast a temple too, and full as dear
As that of Sion ; and as full of sin—
Nothing but thieves and robbers dwell therein ;
Enter, and chase them forth, and cleanse the
    floor,
Crucify them that they may never more
    Profane that holy place
    Where Thou hast chose to set Thy face.
And then if our still tongues shall be
Mute in the praises of Thy deity,
    The stones out of the temple-wall
    Shall cry aloud and call
Hosannah ! and Thy glorious footsteps greet.

A PRAYER FOR CHARITY

Thou, who taught'st the blind man's night
To entertain a double light,
Thine and the day's (and that Thine too)—
The lame away his crutches threw;
The parched crust of leprosy
Returned into its infancy;
The dumb amazed was to hear
His own unchained tongue strike his ear;
Thy powerful mercy did even chase
The devil from his usurped place,
Where Thou Thyself should dwell, not he—
O let Thy love our pattern be;
Let Thy mercy teach one brother
To forgive and love another;
That copying Thy mercy here,
Thy goodness may hereafter rear
Our souls unto Thy glory, when
Our dust shall cease to be with men.

Bishop Jeremy Taylor.

AFFLICTION

The pilot's skill how can we know
    Till tempests blow?
How is that soldier's valour seen
    Which ne'er hath been
In fight? they scarce true soldiers are
That have no wound to show, or scar.

Those soldiers which the general
    Calls out of all
His army to attempt some great
    And brave exploit,
Are those sure whom he means to grace
With honour, and some higher place.

Except we fight, there is no crown
    And no renown;
Unless we sweat in the vineyard,
    There's no reward:
Unless we climb Mount Calvary,
Mount Olivet we shall not see.
              Alexander Rosse.

A GENERAL SONG OF PRAISE TO ALMIGHTY GOD

How shall I sing that Majesty
    Which angels do admire?
Let dust in dust and silence lie;
    Sing, sing, ye heavenly choir.
Thousands of thousands stand around
    Thy throne, O God most high;
Ten thousand times ten thousand sound
    Thy praise; but who am I?

Thy brightness unto them appears,
    Whilst I Thy footsteps trace;
A sound of God comes to my ears;
    But they behold Thy face.
They sing because Thou art their sun:
    Lord, send a beam on me;
For where heaven is but once begun
    There hallelujahs be.

Enlighten with faith's light my heart,
    Enflame it with love's fire;
Then shall I sing and bear a part
    With that celestial choir.

I shall, I fear, be dark and cold,
    With all my fire and light;
Yet when Thou dost accept their gold,
    Lord, treasure up my mite.

How great a being, Lord, is Thine
    Which doth all beings keep!
Thy knowledge is the only line
    To sound so vast a deep.
Thou art a sea without a shore,
    A sun without a sphere;
Thy time is now and evermore,
    Thy place is everywhere.

How good art Thou, whose goodness is
    Our parent, nurse, and guide!
Whose streams do water Paradise,
    And all the earth beside!
Thine upper and Thy nether streams
    Make bold Thy worlds to thrive;
Under Thy warm and sheltering wings
    Thou keep'st two broods alive.

Thy arm of might, most mighty King,
    Both rocks and hearts doth break:
My God, Thou canst do everything
    But what should show Thee weak.
Thou canst not cross Thyself, or be
    Less than Thyself, or poor;
But whatsoever pleaseth Thee
    That canst Thou do, and more.

Who would not fear Thy searching eye,
    Witness to all that's true?
Dark Hell and deep hypocrisy
    Lie plain before its view.
Motions and thoughts before they grow
    Thy knowledge doth espy;
What unborn ages are to do,
    Is done before Thine eye.

Thy bright back-parts, O God of grace,
    I humbly here adore:
Show me Thy glory and Thy face,
    That I may praise Thee more.
Since none can see Thy face and live,
    For me to die is best:
Through Jordan's streams who would not dive,
    To land at Canaan's rest?

"THERE REMAINETH A REST"

My Lord, my Love, was crucified;
    He all the pains did bear;
But in the sweetness of His rest
    He makes His servants share.
How sweetly rest Thy saints above
    Which in Thy bosom lie!
The Church below doth rest in hope
    Of that felicity.

Thou, Lord, who daily feed'st Thy sheep,
   Mak'st them a weekly feast;
Thy flocks meet in their several folds
   Upon this day of rest:
Welcome and dear unto my soul
   Are these sweet feasts of love:
But what a sabbath shall I keep
   When I shall rest above!

I bless Thy wise and wondrous love,
   Which binds us to be free;
Which makes us leave our earthly snares,
   That we may come to Thee!
I come, I wait, I hear, I pray!
   Thy footsteps, Lord, I trace!
I sing to think this is the way
   Unto my Saviour's face!

THE PEACE OF GOD

The world can neither give nor take,
   Nor can they comprehend
The peace of God which Christ has bought,
   The peace which knows no end.

The burning bush was not consumed
   Whilst God remainèd there;
The three, when Jesus made the fourth,
   Found fire as soft as air.

God's furnace doth in Zion stand ;
  But Zion's God sits by,
As the refiner views his gold
  With an observant eye.

His thoughts are high, His love is wise,
  His wounds a cure intend ;
And though He does not always smile,
  He loves unto the end.

John Mason.

THE HOUSE OF THE MIND

As earth's pageant passes by,
Let reflection turn thine eye
Inward, and observe thy breast ;
There alone dwells solid rest.

That's a close immured tower
Which can mock all hostile power :
To thyself a tenant be,
And inhabit safe and free.

Say not that this house is small,
Girt up in a narrow wall ;
In a cleanly sober mind
Heaven itself full room doth find.

Th' infinite Creator can
Dwell in it, and may not man ?
Here content make thy abode
With thyself and with thy God.
Joseph Beaumont.

RESOLUTION

Collect thy soul into one sphere
Of light, and 'bove the earth it rear:
Those wild scatter'd thoughts that erst
Lay loosely in the world dispersed,
Call in: thy spirit thus knit in one
Fair lucid orb, thy fears be gone
Like vain impostures of the night
That fly before the morning bright.
Then with pure eyes thou shalt behold
How the First Goodness doth infold
All things in loving tender arms;
That deemèd mischiefs are no harms,
But sovereign salves and skilful cures
Of greater woes the world endures;
That man's stout soul may win a state
Far raised above the reach of Fate.

Then wilt thou say, *God rules the world*,
Though mountain over mountain hurled
Be pitch'd amid the foaming main,
Which busy winds to wrath constrain;
Though inward tempests fiercely rock
The tott'ring earth, that with the shock
High spires and heavy rocks fall down,
With their own weight drove into ground;

Though pitchy blasts from hell upborne
Stop the outgoings of the morn,
And Nature play her fiery games
In this forced night with fulgurant flames;
Baring by fits for more affright
The pale dead visages, ghastly sight,
Of men astonish'd at the stoure
Of heaven's great rage, the rattling shower
Of hail, the hoarse bellowing of thunder,
Their own loud shrieks made mad with wonder:
All this confusion cannot move
The purgèd mind, freed from the love
Of commerce with her body dear,
Cell of sad thoughts, sole spring of fear.

Power, Wisdom, Goodness sure did frame
This universe and still guide the same.
But thoughts from passions sprung, deceive
Vain mortals. No man can contrive
A better course than what's been run
Since the first circuit of the sun.

He that beholds all from on high
Knows better what to do than I.
I'm not mine own: should I repine
If He dispose of what's not mine?
Purge but thy soul of blind self-will,
Thou straight shall see God doth no ill.
The world He fills with the bright rays
Of His free goodness. He displays

Himself throughout.   Like common air
That Spirit of Life through all doth fare,
Sucked in by them as vital breath
That willingly embrace not death.
But those that with that living law
Be unacquainted, cares do gnaw;
Mistrust of God's good providence
Doth daily vex their wearied sense.

THE PHILOSOPHER'S DEVOTION

Sing aloud! His praise rehearse
Who hath made the universe.
He the boundless heavens has spread,
All the vital orbs has kned,[1]
He that on Olympus high
Tends his flocks with watchful eye,
And this eye [2] hath multiplied
'Midst each flock [3] for to reside.
Thus, as round about they stray,
Toucheth [4] each with outstretched ray;
Nimble they hold on their way,
Shaping out their night and day.
Summer, winter, autumn, spring,
Their inclined axes bring.
Never slack they; none respires,
Dancing round their central fires.

[1] Kneaded.   [2] Sun.
[3] System.   [4] They touch each other.

In due order as they move,
Echoes sweet be gently drove
Thorough heaven's vast hollowness,
Which unto all corners press :
Fills the listening sailers' ears
Riding on the wandering spheres :
Neither speech nor language is
Where their voice is not transmiss.

God is good, is wise, is strong,
Witness all the creature throng,
Is confessed by every tongue ;
All things back[1] from whence they sprung,
As the thankful rivers pay
What they borrowed of the sea.

Now myself I do resign :
Take me whole : I all am Thine.
Save me, God, from self-desire,—
Death's pit, dark hell's raging fire—
Envy, hatred, vengeance, ire :
Let not lust my soul bemire.

Quit from these, Thy praise I'll sing,
Loudly sweep the trembling string.
Bear a part, O Wisdom's sons,
Freed from vain religions !
Lo, from far, I you salute,
Sweetly warbling on my lute—
India, Egypt, Araby,
Asia, Greece, and Tartary.

[1] Go back.

Carmel-tracts, and Lebanon,
With the Mountains of the Moon,
From whence muddy Nile doth run,
Or wherever else you won : [1]
Breathing in one vital air,
One we are, though distant far.

Rise at once, let's sacrifice ;
Odours sweet perfume the skies ;
See how heavenly lightning fires
Hearts inflamed with high aspires !
All the substance of our souls
Up in clouds of incense rolls.
Leave we nothing to ourselves
Save a voice—what need we else !—
Or an hand to wear and tire
On the thankful lute or lyre !

Sing aloud—His praise rehearse
Who hath made the universe.
Henry More.

[1] Dwell.

THE EXIT

My soul, go boldly forth,
Forsake this sinful earth,
What hath it been to thee
   But pain and sorrow,
And think'st thou it will be
   Better to-morrow?

Why art thou for delay?
Thou cam'st not here to stay:
What tak'st thou for thy part
   But heavenly pleasure?
Where then should be thy heart
   But where's thy treasure?

There I shall know God more,
There is the blessed chore,[1]
No wickedness comes there,
   All there is holy:
There is no grief or fear,
   No sin or folly.

Love flames in every breast
The greatest and the least,

[1] Choir.

Strangers to this sweet life
  There are not any.
Love leaves no place for strife,
  Makes one of many.

Each is to other dear ;
No malice enters there,
No siding difference.
  No hurt, no evil ;
Because no ignorance,
  No sin, no devil.

What joy must there needs be
Where all God's glory see,
Feeling God's vital love
  Which still is burning ;
And flaming Godward move,
  Full love returning.

Gladly, my soul, go forth ;
Is heaven of no more worth,
Than this curst desert is,
  This world of trouble ?
Prefer eternal bliss
  Before this bubble.

Wish not still for delay ;
Why would'st thou longer stay
From Christ, from home so far,
  In self-denial :
And live in longer war
  A life of trial ?

Cherish not causeless doubt
That God will shut thee out:
What if He thee assured
   From heaven by letter?
His Son, His Spirit, and Word
   Have done it better.

Christ who knows all His sheep
Will all in safety keep.
He will not lose His blood
   Nor intercession:
Nor we the purchased good
   Of His dear Passion.

I know my God is just,
To Him I wholly trust
All that I have and am,
   All that I hope for:
All's sure and seen to Him
   Which I here grope for.

Lord Jesus, take my Spirit,
I trust Thy love and merit:
Take home this wandering sheep,
   For Thou hast sought it:
This soul in safety keep,
   For Thou hast bought it. Amen.

Richard Baxter.

A DIALOGUE between the RESOLVED SOUL and CREATED PLEASURE

Courage, my soul! now learn to wield
The weight of thine immortal shield;
Close on thy head thy helmet bright;
Balance thy sword against the fight;
See where an army, strong as fair,
With silken banners spreads the air!
Now, if thou be'st that thing divine,
In this day's combat let it shine,
And show that nature wants an art
To conquer one resolvèd heart.

Pleasure. Welcome the creation's guest,
Lord of earth, and heaven's heir!
Lay aside that warlike crest,
And of nature's banquet share;
Where the souls of fruits and flowers
Stand prepared to heighten yours.

Soul. I sup above, and cannot stay
    To bait so long upon the way.

Pleasure. On these downy pillows lie,
    Whose soft plumes will thither fly:
    On these roses, strewed so plain
    Lest one leaf thy side should strain.

Soul. My gentler rest is on a thought,
    Conscious of doing what I ought.

Pleasure. If thou be'st with perfumes pleased,
    Such as oft the gods appeased,
    Thou in fragrant clouds shalt show,
    Like another god below.

Soul. A soul that knows not to presume,
    Is heaven's, and it's own, perfume.

Pleasure. Everything does seem to vie
    Which should first attract thine eye:
    But since none deserves that grace,
    In this crystal view thy face.

Soul. When the Creator's skill is prized,
    The rest is all but earth disguised.

Pleasure. Hark, how music then prepares
    For thy stay these charming airs,
    Which the posting winds recall,
    And suspend the river's fall.

Soul. Had I but any time to lose,
On this I would it all dispose.
Cease, tempter! None can chain a mind,
Whom this sweet cordage cannot bind.

Chorus. Earth cannot show so brave a sight,
As when a single soul does fence
The batteries of alluring sense,
And heaven views it with delight.
Then persevere; for still new charges sound,
And if thou overcom'st thou shalt be crowned.

Pleasure. All that's costly, fair, and sweet,
Which scatteringly doth shine,
Shall within one beauty meet,
And she be only thine.

Soul. If things of sight such heavens be,
What heavens are those we cannot see?

Pleasure. Wheresoe'er thy foot shall go
The minted gold shall lie,
Till thou purchase all below,
And want new worlds to buy.

Soul. Wer't not for price, who'd value gold?
      And that's worth naught that can be sold.

Pleasure. Wilt thou all the glory have
        That war or peace commend?
      Half the world shall be thy slave,
        The other half thy friend.

Soul. What friend, if to myself untrue?
      What slaves, unless I captive you?

Pleasure. Thou shalt know each hidden cause,
        And see the future time;
      Try what depth the centre draws,
        And then to heaven climb.

Soul. None thither mounts by the degree
      Of knowledge, but humility.

Chorus. Triumph, triumph, victorious soul!
        The world has not one pleasure more:
      The rest does lie beyond the pole,
        And is thine everlasting store.

ON A DROP OF DEW

SEE, how the orient dew,
Shed from the bosom of the morn
    Into the blowing roses
(Yet careless of its mansion new,

For the clear region where 'twas born),
   Round in itself encloses;
And in its little globe's extent,
Frames, as it can, its native element.
  How it the purple flower does slight,
    Scarce touching where it lies;
  But gazing back upon the skies,
    Shines with a mournful light,
      Like its own tear,
Because so long divided from the sphere.
  Restless it rolls, and unsecure,
    Trembling, lest it grow impure;
  Till the warm sun pity its pain,
And to the skies exhale it back again.
  So the soul, that drop, that ray
   Of the clear fountain of eternal day
(Could it within the human flower be seen),
    Remembering still its former height,
     Shuns the sweet leaves, and blossoms green,
    And, recollecting its own light,
Does in its pure and circling thoughts express
The greater heaven in an heaven less.
   In how coy a figure wound,
    Every way it turns away;
   So the world excluding round,
    Yet receiving in the day;
    Dark beneath, but bright above,
    Here disdaining, there in love.
  How loose and easy hence to go;
  How girt and ready to ascend;

    Moving but on a point below,
    It all about does upwards bend.
Such did the manna's sacred dew distil ;
White and entire, though congealed and chill ;
Congealed on earth ; but does, dissolving, run
Into the glories of the Almighty sun.
Andrew Marvell.

MATTINS

When first thy eyes unveil, give thy soul leave
To do the like ; our bodies but fore-run
The spirit's duty ; true hearts spread and heave
Unto their God as flowers do to the sun.
 Give Him thy first thoughts then, so shalt
  thou keep
 Him company all day, and in Him sleep.

Walk with thy fellow-creatures : note the hush
And whispers amongst them. There's not a
 spring
Or leaf but hath his morning hymn. Each
 bush
And oak doth know I AM. Canst thou not
 sing ?
 O leave thy cares and follies ! go this way ;
 And thou art sure to prosper all the day.

MAN

 Weighing the steadfastness and state
Of some mean things which here below reside,
Where birds like watchful clocks the noiseless
 date
 And intercourse of times divide,

Where bees at night get home and hive, and
      flow'rs,
         Early as well as late,
Rise with the sun, and set in the same bow'rs,

   I would, said I, my God would give
The staidness of these things to man! for these
To His divine appointments ever cleave,
   And no new business breaks their peace;
The birds nor sow nor reap, yet sup and dine,
         The flow'rs without clothes live,
Yet Solomon was never drest so fine.

   Man hath still either toys or care;
He hath no root, nor to one place is tied,
But ever restless and irregular
   About this earth doth run and ride.
He knows he hath a home, but scarce knows
      where;
         He says it is so far,
That he hath quite forgot how to go there.

   He knocks at all doors, strays and roams:
Nay, hath not so much wit as some stones have,
Which in the darkest nights point to their
      homes
   By some hid sense their Maker gave;
Man is the shuttle, to whose winding quest
         And passage through these looms
God order'd motion, but ordain'd no rest.

THE RETREAT

Happy those early days, when I
Shined in my angel-infancy!
Before I understood this place
Appointed for my second race,
Or taught my soul to fancy ought
But a white, celestial thought;
When yet I had not walk'd above
A mile or two from my first Love,
And looking back, at that short space,
Could see a glimpse of His bright face;
When on some gilded Cloud or Flow'r
My gazing soul would dwell an hour,
And in those weaker glories spy
Some shadows of eternity;
Before I taught my tongue to wound
My conscience with a sinful sound,
Or had the black art to dispense
A sev'ral sin to ev'ry sense,
But felt through all this fleshly dress
Bright shoots of everlastingness.
  O how I long to travel back,
And tread again that ancient track!
That I might once more reach that plain,
Where first I left my glorious train;
From whence th' enlightened spirit sees
That shady city of palm trees.
But ah! my soul with too much stay
Is drunk, and staggers in the way.

Some men a forward motion love,
But I by backward steps would move;
And, when this dust falls to the urn,
In that state I came, return.

ETENIM RES CREATÆ EXERTO CAPITE OBSERVANTES EXPECTANT REVELATIONEM FILIORUM DEI

And do they so? have they a sense
  Of ought but influence?
Can they their heads lift, and expect,
  And groan too? why th' elect,
Can do no more: my volumes said
  They were all dull, and dead;
They judged them senseless, and their state
  Wholly inanimate.
  Go, go; seal up thy looks,
   And burn thy books.

I would I were a stone, or tree,
  Or flow'r by pedigree,
Or some poor highway herb, or spring
  To flow, or bird to sing!
Then should I, tied to one sure state,
  All day expect my date.
But I am sadly loose, and stray
  A giddy blast each way;
  O let me not thus range!
   Thou canst not change.

Sometimes I sit with Thee, and tarry
    An hour or so, then vary.
Thy other creatures in this scene
    Thee only aim and mean;
Some rise to seek Thee, and with heads
    Erect peep from their beds;
Others, whose birth is in the tomb,
    And cannot quit the womb,
    Sigh there, and groan for Thee,
    Their liberty.

O let not me do less! shall they
    Watch, while I sleep or play?
Shall I Thy mercies still abuse
    With fancies, friends, or news?
O brook it not! Thy blood is mine,
    And my soul should be Thine;
O brook it not! why wilt Thou stop
    After whole show'rs one drop?
    Sure Thou wilt joy to see
    Thy sheep with Thee.

DESERT

I HAVE deserved a thick Egyptian damp,
    Dark as my deeds,
Should mist within me, and put out that lamp
    Thy spirit feeds;

A darting conscience full of stabs and fears ;
    No shade but yew,
Sullen and sad eclipses, cloudy spheres,
    These are my due.
But He that with His blood, a price too dear,
    My scores did pay,
Bid me, by virtue from Him, challenge here
    The brightest day ;
Sweet, downy thoughts, soft lily-shades, calm streams,
    Joys full and true,
Fresh spicy mornings and eternal beams,
    These are His due.

LOVE AND DISCIPLINE

Since in a land not barren still,
Because Thou dost Thy grace distil,
My lot is fallen, blest be Thy will

And since these biting frosts but kill
Some tares in me which choke or spill
That seed Thou sow'st, blest be Thy skill !

Blest be Thy dew, and blest Thy frost,
And happy I to be so crost
And cured by crosses at Thy cost.

The dew doth cheer what is distrest,
The frosts ill weeds nip and molest,
In both Thou work'st unto the best.

Thus while Thy several mercies plot,
And work on me, now cold, now hot,
The work goes on and slacketh not;

For as Thy hand the weather steers,
So thrive I best 'twixt joys and tears,
And all the year have some green ears.

LIBERTY

Lord, bind me up, and let me lie
A prisoner to my liberty,
If such a state at all can be
As an imprisonment serving Thee;
The wind, though gathered in Thy fist,
Yet doth it blow still where it list,
And yet shouldst Thou let go Thy hold,
Those gusts might quarrel and grow bold.
   As waters here, headlong and loose,
The lower grounds still chase and choose,
Where spreading all the way they seek
And search out every hole and creek;
So my spilt thoughts, winding from Thee,
Take the down-road to vanity,
Where they all stray and strive, which shall
Find out the first and steepest fall.

THE WORLD

Thou art not Truth ! for he that tries
Shall find thee all deceit and lies.
Thou art not Friendship ! for in thee
'Tis but the bait of policy ;
Which like a viper lodged in flowers
Its venom through that sweetness pours.
And when not so, then always 'tis
A fading paint, the short-lived bliss
Of air and humour, out and in,
Like colours in a dolphin's skin.
Thou art not Riches ! for that trash,
Which one age hoards, the next doth wash
And so severely sweep away,
That few remember where it lay.
So rapid streams the wealthy land
About them have at their command,
And shifting channels here restore,
There break down what they bank'd before
Thou art not Honour ! for those gay
Feathers will wear and drop away ;
And princes to some upstart line
Give new ones that are full as fine.
Thou art not Pleasure ! For thy rose
Upon a thorn doth still repose,
Which, if not cropt, will quickly shed,
But soon as cropt grows dull and dead.
   Thou art the sand which fills one glass,
And then doth to another pass ;

And could I put thee to a stay,
Thou art but dust.   Then go thy way,
And leave me clean and bright though poor ;
Who stops thee doth but daub his floor ;
And, swallow-like, when he hath done,
To unknown dwellings must be gone.

PROVIDENCE

Sacred and secret hand !
By whose assisting, swift command
The angel showed that holy well,
Which freed poor Hagar from her fears,
And turned to smiles the begging tears
Of young distressed Ishmael.

If I Thy servant be,
Whose service makes ev'n captives free,
A fish shall all my tribute pay,
The swift-wing'd raven shall bring me meat,
And I, like flowers, shall still go neat,
As if I knew no month but May.

Poor birds this doctrine sing ;
And herbs, which on dry hills do spring
Or in the howling wilderness,
Do know Thy dewy morning hours,
And watch all night for mists and showers,
Then drink and praise Thy bounteousness.

THE RAINBOW

Still young and fine ! but what is still in view
We slight as old and soil'd, though fresh and new.
How bright wert thou, when Shem's admiring eye
Thy burnisht flaming arch did first descry !
When Terah, Nahor, Haran, Abram, Lot,
The youthful world's grey fathers in one knot,
Did with intentive looks watch every hour
For thy new light, and trembled at each shower !
When thou dost shine, darkness looks white and fair,
Storms turn to music, clouds to smiles and air,
Rain gently spends his honey-drops, and pours
Balm on the cleft earth, milk on grass and flowers.
Bright pledge of peace and sunshine ! the sure tie
Of thy Lord's hand, the object of His eye !
When I behold thee, though my light be dim,
Distant, and low, I can in thine see Him,
Who looks upon thee from His glorious throne,
And minds the covenant 'twixt all and One.

THE NIGHT

Through that pure Virgin-shrine,
That sacred veil drawn o'er thy glorious noon,
That men might look and live, as glow-worms shine,
    And face the moon,
Wise Nicodemus saw such light
As made him know his God by night.

Most blest believer he!
Who in that land of darkness and blind eyes
Thy long-expected healing wings could see,
    When Thou didst rise;
And, what can never more be done,
Did at midnight speak with the Sun!

O who will tell me where
He found Thee at that dead and silent hour!
What hallow'd solitary ground did bear
    So rare a flower;
Within whose sacred leaves did lie
The fulness of the Deity!

No mercy seat of gold,
No dead and dusty cherub, nor carved stone,
But His own living works, did my Lord hold
    And lodge alone;
Where trees and herbs did watch and peep
And wonder, while the Jews did sleep.

    Dear night! this world's defeat;
The stop to busy fools; care's check and curb;
The day of spirits; my soul's calm retreat
        Which none disturb!
    Christ's progress, and His prayer time;
    The hours to which high heaven doth chime;

    God's silent, searching flight;
When my Lord's head is filled with dew, and all
His locks are wet with the clear drops of night
        His still, soft call;
    His knocking time; the soul's dumb watch,
    When spirits their fair kindred catch.

    Were all my loud, evil days
Calm and unhaunted as is thy dark tent,
Whose peace but by some Angel's wing or voice
        Is seldom rent;
    Then I in heaven all the long year
    Would keep, and never wander here.

    But living where the sun
Doth all things wake, and where all mix and tire
Themselves and others, I consent and run
        To every mire;
    And by this world's ill-guiding light,
    Err more than I can do by night.

There is in God, some say,
A deep but dazzling darkness; as men here
Say it is late and dusky, because they
    See not all clear.
  O for that night! where I in Him
  Might live invisible and dim!

DEPARTED FRIENDS

THEY are all gone into the world of light!
    And I alone sit lingering here!
Their very memory is fair and bright,
    And my sad thoughts doth clear.

It glows and glitters in my cloudy breast
    Like stars upon some gloomy grove,
Or those faint beams in which this hill is drest
    After the sun's remove.

I see them walking in an air of glory,
    Whose light doth trample on my days;
My days, which are at best but dull and hoary,
    Mere glimmering and decays.

O holy Hope! and high Humility!
    High as the heavens above;
These are your walks, and you have show'd them me
    To kindle my cold love.

Dear, beauteous death ; the jewel of the just !
    Shining nowhere but in the dark ;
What mysteries do lie beyond thy dust,
        Could man outlook that mark !

He that hath found some fledged bird's nest may know
    At first sight if the bird be flown ;
But what fair well or grove he sings in now,
        That is to him unknown.

And yet, as angels in some brighter dreams
    Call to the soul when man doth sleep,
So some strange thoughts transcend our wonted themes
        And into glory peep.

If a star were confined into a tomb,
    Her captive flames must needs burn there ;
But when the hand that lock'd her up gives room,
        She'll shine through all the sphere.

O Father of eternal life, and all
    Created glories under Thee !
Resume Thy spirit from this world of thrall
        Into true liberty !

Either disperse these mists, which blot and fill
    My perspective still as they pass ;
Or else remove me hence unto that hill,
        Where I shall need no glass.

THE DAWNING

Ah! what time wilt Thou come? when shall
    that cry,
The Bridegroom's coming! fill the sky;
Shall it in the evening run
When our words and works are done?
Or will Thy all-surprising light
        Break at midnight,
When either sleep or some dark pleasure
Possesseth mad man without measure?
Or shall these early, fragrant hours
        Unlock Thy bow'rs,
And with their blush of light descry
Thy locks crown'd with eternity?
Indeed, it is the only time
That with Thy glory doth best chime;
All now are stirring, ev'ry field
        Full hymns doth yield;
The whole Creation shakes off night,
And for Thy shadow looks the light;
Stars now vanish without number,
Sleepy planets set and slumber,
The pursy clouds disband and scatter,
All expect some sudden matter;
Not one beam triumphs but from far
        That morning-star.

O at what time soever Thou
Unknown to us the heavens wilt bow,

And, with Thy angels in the van,
Descend to judge poor careless man,
Grant, I may not like puddle lie
In a corrupt security,
Where if a traveller water crave,
He finds it dead, and in a grave.
But as this restless, vocal spring
All day and night doth run, and sing,
And though here born, yet is acquainted
Elsewhere, and flowing keeps untainted ;
So let me all my busy age
In Thy free services engage ;
And though (while here) of force I must
Have commerce sometimes with poor dust,
And in my flesh, though vile and low,
As this doth in her channel flow,
Yet let my course, my aim, my love,
And chief acquaintance be above ;
So when that day and hour shall come,
In which Thyself will be the sun,
Thou'lt find me drest and on my way,
Watching the break of Thy great day.

Henry Vaughan.

THE SHEPHERD BOY'S SONG IN THE VALLEY OF HUMILIATION

He that is down needs fear no fall,
   He that is low no pride;
He that is humble ever shall
   Have God to be his guide.

I am content with what I have,
   Little be it or much;
And, Lord, contentment still I crave
   Because Thou savest such.

Fulness to such a burden is
   That go on pilgrimage;
Here little and hereafter bliss
   Is best from age to age.
                    John Bunyan.

THE ASPIRATION

    How long, great God, how long must I
      Immured in this dark prison lie;
Where at the grates and avenues of sense,
My soul must watch to have intelligence;
Where but faint gleams of Thee salute my sight,
Like doubtful moonshine in a cloudy night;
      When shall I leave this magic sphere,
      And be all mind, all eye, all ear?

      How cold this clime! And yet my sense
      Perceives e'en here Thy influence.
E'en here Thy strong magnetic charms I feel,
And pant and tremble like the amorous steel.
To lower good, and beauties less divine,
Sometimes my erroneous needle does incline;
      But yet, so strong the sympathy,
      It turns and points again to Thee.

      I long to see this excellence
      Which at such distance strikes my sense.
My impatient soul struggles to disengage
Her wings from the confinement of her cage.
Would'st Thou, great Love, this prisoner once set free,
How would she hasten to be link'd to Thee!
      She'd for no angel's conduct stay,
      But fly, and love on all the way.
                      John Norris.

FOR CHRISTMAS

And art Thou come, blest Babe, and come to me?
Come down to teach me how to come to Thee?
Welcome, thrice welcome, to my panting soul,
Which, as it loves, doth grieve that 'tis so foul.
The less 'tis fit for Thee come from above,
The more it needs Thee, and the more I love.

But art Thou come, dear Saviour? hath Thy love
Thus made Thee stoop, and leave Thy throne above,
Thy lofty heavens, and thus Thyself to dress
In dust to visit mortals? Could no less
A condescension serve, and after all
The mean reception of a cratch and stall?
Dear Lord, I'll fetch Thee hence! I have a room—
'Tis poor, but 'tis my best—if Thou wilt come
Within so small a cell, where I would fain
Mine and the world's Redeemer entertain.
I mean my heart; 'tis sluttish, I confess,
And will not mend Thy lodging, Lord, unless
Thou send before Thy harbinger, I mean
Thy pure and purging Grace, to make it clean,
And sweep its nasty corners; then I'll try
To wash it also with a weeping eye.

And when 'tis swept and wash'd, I then will go
And with Thy leave I'll fetch some flowers that
    grow
In thine own garden, Faith and Love, to Thee;
With these I'll dress it up, and these shall be
My rosemary and bays.   Yet when my best
Is done, the room's not fit for such a guest:
But here's the cure; Thy presence, Lord, alone
Will make a stall a Court, a cratch a Throne.

LITANY

Lamb of God, my Saviour!
    Explain before me
Thy matchless love, and by Thy grace procure me
    A mind like Thine.

Thy humiliation
    In leaving heaven,
In being poor, and to a stable driven,
    Teach me to stoop.

Thy birth of a Virgin
    Make me live chastely
Unspotted from the world, and manifestly
    Sealed for the Lord.

Thy flight into Egypt
    In such great danger
Teach me to be a pilgrim here and stranger
    In every place.

Thine innocent childhood
  And meek behaviour
Teach me to be a little child for ever
  Before Thy face.

Thy wondrous obedience
  And true subjection
Unto Thy parents, melt to like affection
  My stubborn heart.

Thy carpenter's labour,
  Thy work and travel,
Daily preserve my handy-work from evil,
  And bless my toil.

Thy goodwill to all men
  By Thee created
Teach me to honour all and tender-hearted
  Behave to all.

Thy forty days' fasting,
  Thy self-denial,
Thy being sorely tried, in every trial
  Deliver me.

THE WAYS OF WISDOM

These sweeter far than lilies are,
No roses may with these compare :
 How these excel
 No tongue can tell,

Which he that well and truly knows
    With praise and joy he goes!
How great and happy's he that knows his ways
    To be divine and heavenly joys;
    To whom each city is more brave
Than walls of pearl, and streets which gold doth pave;
    Whose open eyes
    Behold the skies,
Who loves their wealth and beauty more
    Than kings love golden ore!

Who sees the heavenly ancient ways
Of God the Lord, with joy and praise
    More than the skies;
    With open eyes
Doth prize them all; yea, more than gems,
    And regal diadems;
That more esteemeth mountains, as they are,
    Than if they gold and silver were:
    To whom the sun more pleasure brings,
Than crowns, and thrones, and palaces to kings;
    That knows his ways
    To be the joys
And way of God. These things who knows
    With joy and praise he goes!

THE CHILD'S DEATH

He did but float a little way
  Adown the stream of time;
With dreamy eyes watching the ripples play,
  Or listening to their chime.
      His slender sail
      Scarce felt the gale;
He did but float a little way,
And, putting to the shore,
While yet 'twas early day,
Went calmly on his way,
      To dwell with us no more.
No jarring did he feel,
No grating on his vessel's keel;
A strip of yellow sand
Mingled the waters with the land,
Where he was seen no more;
O stern word, Never more!
Full short his journey was; no dust
  Of earth unto his sandals clave;
The weary weight, that old men must,
    He bore not to the grave.
He seem'd a cherub who had lost his way
And wander'd hither; so his stay
With us was short; and 'twas most meet
  That he should be no delver in earth's clod,
Nor need to pause and cleanse his feet
  To stand before his God.

Anon.

AN ODE

The spacious firmament on high,
With all the blue ethereal sky,
And spangled heavens, a shining frame,
Their great Original proclaim.
The unwearied sun, from day to day,
Does his Creator's power display;
And publishes to every land
The work of an Almighty hand.

Soon as the evening shades prevail,
The moon takes up the wondrous tale,
And nightly to the listening earth
Repeats the story of her birth;
Whilst all the stars that round her burn,
And all the planets in their turn,
Confirm the tidings as they roll,
And spread the truth from pole to pole.

What though in solemn silence all
Move round the dark terrestrial ball?
What though no real voice nor sound
Amidst their radiant orbs be found?
In Reason's ear they all rejoice,
And utter forth a glorious voice;
For ever singing as they shine,
The hand that made us is divine.
Joseph Addison.

A SIGHT OF HEAVEN IN SICKNESS

Oft have I sat in secret sighs
   To feel my flesh decay;
Then groan'd aloud with frighted eyes
   To view the tott'ring clay.

But I forbid my sorrows now,
   Nor dares the flesh complain,
Diseases bring their profit too,
   The joy o'ercomes the pain.

My cheerful soul now all the day
   Sits waiting here, and sings;
Looks through the ruins of her clay,
   And practises her wings.

The shines of heaven rush sweetly in
   At all the gaping flaws;
Visions of endless bliss are seen
   And native air she draws.

O may these walls stand tott'ring still,
   The breaches never close,
If I must here in darkness dwell,
   And all this glory lose.

Or rather let this flesh decay,
   The ruins wider grow,
Till, glad to see th' enlarged way,
   I stretch my pinions through.

Had I a glance of Thee, my God,
   Kingdoms and men would vanish soon;
Vanish as though I saw them not,
   As a dim candle dies at noon.

Then they might fight, and rage, and rave,
   I should perceive the noise no more
Than we can hear a shaking leaf,
   While rattling thunders round us roar.

My God, permit me not to be
A stranger to myself and Thee;
Amidst a thousand thoughts I rove,
Forgetful of my highest love.

Be earth with all her scenes withdrawn,
Let noise and vanity begone;
In secret silence of the mind,
My heaven, and there my God, I find.

                Dr. Isaac Watts.

THE DESPONDING SOUL'S WISH

My spirit longeth for Thee,
  Within my troubled breast,
Altho' I be unworthy
  Of so divine a Guest.

Of so divine a Guest,
  Unworthy tho' I be,
Yet has my heart no rest,
  Unless it come from Thee.

Unless it come from Thee,
  In vain I look around;
In all that I can see,
  No rest is to be found.

No rest is to be found,
  But in Thy blessèd love;
O! let my wish be crown'd,
  And send it from above!

THE ANSWER

Cheer up, desponding Soul,
  Thy longing pleased I see;
'Tis part of that great whole,
  Wherewith I longed for thee.

Wherewith I longed for thee,
  And left My Father's throne;
From death to set thee free,
  To claim thee for My own.

To claim thee for My own,
  I suffered on the cross:
Oh, were My love but known,
  No soul could fear its loss.

No soul could fear its loss,
  But filled with love divine,
Would die on its own cross,
  And rise for ever Mine.

THE SOUL'S TENDENCY TOWARDS ITS TRUE CENTRE

Stones towards the earth descend;
  Rivers to the ocean roll;
Every motion has some end:
  What is thine, beloved Soul?

Mine is where my Saviour is;
  There with Him I hope to dwell;
Jesu is the central bliss;
  Love the force that doth impel.

Truly thou hast answered right:
  Now may heaven's attractive grace,
Towards the source of thy delight,
  Speed along thy quickening pace!

DIVINE EPIGRAMS

I.

No faith towards God can e'er subsist with wrath
Towards man, nor charity with want of faith;
From the same root hath each of them its growth;
You have not either if you have not both.

II.

Think, and be careful what thou art within;
For there is sin in the desire of sin:
Think, and be thankful, in a different case:
For there is grace in the desire of grace.

III.

Let thy repentance be without delay—
If thou defer it to another day,
Thou must repent for a day more of sin,
While a day less remains to do it in.

IV.

Hath not the potter power to make his clay
Just what he pleases? Well, and tell me pray,
What kind of potter must we think a man
Who does not make the best of it he can?
Who making some fine vessels of his clay,
To show his power, throws all the rest away,
Which, in itself, was equally as fine?
What an idea this of Power divine!

John Byrom.

WRESTLING WITH THE ANGEL

Come, O Thou Traveller unknown,
   Whom still I hold, but cannot see,
My company before is gone,
   And I am left alone with Thee;
With Thee all night I mean to stay,
And wrestle till the break of day.

I need not tell Thee who I am,
   My misery or sin declare;
Thyself hast call'd me by my name;
   Look on Thy hands and read it there!
But who, I ask Thee, who art Thou?
Tell me Thy name, and tell me now.

In vain Thou strugglest to get free,
   I never will unloose my hold;
Art Thou the Man that died for me?
   The secret of Thy love unfold.
Wrestling, I will not let Thee go,
Till I Thy Name, Thy Nature know.

Wilt Thou not yet to me reveal
   Thy new, unutterable Name?
Tell me, I still beseech Thee, tell:
   To know it now, resolved I am:

Wrestling, I will not let Thee go,
Till I Thy Name, Thy Nature know.

What though my shrinking flesh complain,
    And murmur to contend so long?
I rise superior to my pain;
    When I am weak, then I am strong:
And when my all of strength shall fail,
I shall with the God-Man prevail.

My strength is gone; my nature dies;
    I sink beneath Thy weighty hand;
Faint to revive, and fall to rise;
    I fall, and yet by faith I stand:
I stand, and will not let Thee go,
Till I Thy Name, Thy Nature know.

Yield to me now, for I am weak,
    But confident in self-despair;
Speak to my heart, in blessings speak,
    Be conquer'd by my instant prayer!
Speak, or Thou never hence shalt move,
And tell me, if Thy Name is Love?

'Tis Love! 'tis Love! Thou died'st for me
    I hear Thy whisper in my heart!
The morning breaks, the shadows flee;
    Pure universal Love Thou art!
To me, to all, Thy bowels move;
Thy Nature and Thy Name is Love!

My prayer hath power with God; the grace
   Unspeakable I now receive;
Through faith I see Thee face to face,
   I see Thee face to face, and live:
In vain I have not wept and strove;
Thy Nature and Thy Name is Love.

I know Thee, Saviour, Who Thou art;
   Jesus, the feeble sinner's Friend!
Nor wilt Thou with the night depart,
   But stay, and love me to the end!
Thy mercies never shall remove—
Thy Nature and Thy Name is Love!

The Sun of Righteousness on me
   Hath rose, with healing in His wings;
Wither'd my nature's strength, from Thee
   My soul its life and succour brings;
My help is all laid up above;
Thy Nature and Thy Name is Love.

Contented now upon my thigh
   I halt, till life's short journey end;
All helplessness, all weakness, I
   On Thee alone for strength depend;
Nor have I power from Thee to move;
Thy Nature and Thy Name is Love.

                Charles Wesley.

LIGHT OUT OF DARKNESS

God moves in a mysterious way
    His wonders to perform;
He plants His footsteps in the sea
    And rides upon the storm.

Deep in unfathomable mines
    Of never-failing skill,
He treasures up His bright designs,
    And works His sovereign will.

Ye fearful saints, fresh courage take,
    The clouds ye so much dread
Are big with mercy, and shall break
    In blessings on your head.

Judge not the Lord by feeble sense,
    But trust Him for His grace;
Behind a frowning Providence
    He hides a smiling face.

His purposes will ripen fast,
    Unfolding every hour;
The bud may have a bitter taste,
    But sweet will be the flower.

Blind unbelief is sure to err,
  And scan His work in vain :
God is His own interpreter,
  And He will make it plain.

THE CONTRITE HEART

The Lord will happiness divine
  On contrite hearts bestow ;
Then tell me, gracious God, is mine
  A contrite heart or no.

I hear, but seem to hear in vain,
  Insensible as steel ;
If aught is felt, 'tis only pain,
  To find I cannot feel.

My best desires are faint and few,
  I fain would strive for more ;
But when I cry, " My strength renew ! "
  Seem weaker than before.

O make this heart rejoice or ache,
  Decide this doubt for me;
And if it be not broken, break,—
  And heal it if it be.

William Cowper.

FAITH

O God, whose thunder shakes the sky,
    Whose eye this atom globe surveys,
To Thee, my only rock, I fly,
    Thy mercy in Thy justice praise.

The mystic mazes of Thy will,—
    The shadows of celestial light,—
Are past the power of human skill,
    But what the Eternal acts is right.

Oh, teach me in the trying hour
    When anguish swells the dewy tear,
To still my sorrows, own Thy power,
    Thy goodness love, Thy justice fear.

If in this bosom aught but Thee
    Encroaching sought a boundless sway,
Omniscience could the danger see,
    And mercy look the cause away.

Then why, my soul, dost thou complain?
    Why drooping seek the dark recess?
Shake off the melancholy chain,
    For God created all to bless.

The gloomy mantle of the night,
　Which on my sinking spirit steals,
Will vanish at the morning light,
　Which God, my East, my Sun, reveals.
　　　　　　　　Thomas Chatterton.

THE PILGRIM

Pilgrim, burden'd with thy sin,
Come the way to Zion's gate,
There, till Mercy let thee in,
Knock, and weep, and watch, and wait.
    Knock!—He knows the sinner's cry:
    Weep!—He loves the mourner's tears:
    Watch!—for saving grace is nigh:
    Wait—till heavenly light appears.

Hark! it is the Bridegroom's voice;
Welcome, pilgrim, to thy rest;
Now within the gate rejoice,
Safe, and seal'd, and bought, and blest!
    Safe—from all the lures of vice,
    Seal'd—by signs the chosen know,
    Bought—by love and life the price,
    Blest—the mighty debt to owe.

Holy pilgrim! what for thee
In a world like this remain?
From thy guarded breast shall flee
Fear, and shame, and doubt, and pain.
    Fear—the hope of heaven shall fly,
    Shame—from glory's view retire:
    Doubt—in certain rapture die,
    Pain—in endless bliss expire.
                      George Crabbe.

THE NEW JERUSALEM

I.

ENGLAND, awake! awake! awake!
　　Jerusalem thy sister calls!
Why wilt thou sleep the sleep of death,
　　And close her from thy ancient walls?

Thy hills and valleys felt her feet
　　Gently upon their bosoms move:
Thy gates beheld sweet Zion's ways;
　　Then was a time of joy and love.

And now the time returns again:
　　Our souls exult; and London's towers
Receive the Lamb of God to dwell
　　In England's green and pleasant bowers.

II.

And did those feet in ancient time
　　Walk upon England's mountain green?
And was the holy Lamb of God
　　On England's pleasant pasture seen?

And did the countenance divine
　　Shine forth upon our clouded hills?
And was Jerusalem builded here
　　Among these dark Satanic mills?

Bring me my bow of burning gold !
   Bring me my arrows of desire !
Bring me my spear : O clouds, unfold !
   Bring me my chariot of fire !

I will not cease from mental fight,
   Nor shall my sword sleep in my hand,
Till we have built Jerusalem
   In England's green and pleasant land.

THE TWO SONGS

I HEARD an Angel singing
When the day was springing :
" Mercy, pity, and peace
Are the world's release."
So he sang all day
Over the new-mown hay,
Till the sun went down,
And haycocks looked brown.

I heard a Devil curse
Over the heath and the furse :
" Mercy could be no more
If there were nobody poor,
And pity no more could be
If all were happy as ye :
And mutual fear brings peace.
Misery's increase
Are mercy, pity, peace."
At his curse the sun went down,
And the heavens gave a frown.

AUGURIES OF INNOCENCE

To see a world in a grain of sand,
  And a heaven in a wild flower;
Hold infinity in the palm of your hand,
  And eternity in an hour.

A robin redbreast in a cage
Puts all heaven in a rage;
A skylark wounded on the wing
Doth make a cherub cease to sing.
Kill not the moth nor butterfly,
For the last judgment draweth nigh.

He who respects the infant's faith
Triumphs over hell and death.
He who shall teach the child to doubt
The rotting grave shall ne'er get out.
He who replies to words of doubt
Doth put the light of knowledge out;
A puddle, or the cricket's cry,
Is to doubt a fit reply.

Every night and every morn
Some to misery are born;
Every morn and every night
Some are born to sweet delight.
Joy and woe are woven fine,
A clothing for the soul divine;
Under every grief and pine
Runs a joy with silken twine.

God appears, and God is light
To those poor souls who dwell in night;
But doth a human form display
To those who dwell in realms of day.

DIVINE EPIGRAMS

I.

A TEAR is an intellectual thing,
And a sigh is the sword of an angel king,
And the bitter groan of a martyr's woe
Is an arrow from the Almighty's bow.

II.

I was angry with my friend:
I told my wrath, my wrath did end.
I was angry with my foe:
I told it not, my wrath did grow.

III.

Mutual forgiveness of each vice
Such are the gates of paradise.

IV.

The door of death is made of gold
That mortal eyes can not behold;
But when the mortal eyes are closed,
And cold and pale the limbs reposed,
The soul awakes, and wondering sees
In her mild hand the golden keys.

William Blake.

ODE TO DUTY

Stern Daughter of the Voice of God !
O Duty ! if that name thou love,
Who art a light to guide, a rod
To check the erring, and reprove ;
Thou, who art victory and law
When empty terrors overawe,
From vain temptations dost set free ;
And calm'st the weary strife of frail humanity !

There are who ask not if thine eye
Be on them ; who, in love and truth,
Where no misgiving is, rely
Upon the genial sense of youth :
Glad hearts ! without reproach or blot ;
Who do thy work, and know it not :
Long may the kindly impulse last !
But thou, if they should totter, teach them to stand fast !

Serene will be our days and bright,
And happy will our nature be,
When love is an unerring light,
And joy its own security.
And they a blissful course may hold
Even now, who, not unwisely bold,
Live in the spirit of this creed ;
Yet seek thy firm support, according to their need.

I, loving freedom, and untried,
No sport of every random gust,
Yet being to myself a guide,
Too blindly have reposed my trust;
And oft, when in my heart was heard
Thy timely mandate, I deferred
The task, in smoother walks to stray;
But thee I now would serve more strictly, if I may.

Through no disturbance of my soul,
Or strong compunction in me wrought,
I supplicate for thy control;
But in the quietness of thought:
Me this unchartered freedom tires;
I feel the weight of chance-desires:
My hopes no more must change their name,
I long for a repose that ever is the same.

Stern Law-giver! yet thou dost wear
The Godhead's most benignant grace;
Nor know we anything so fair
As is the smile upon thy face:
Flowers laugh before thee on their beds
And fragrance in thy footing treads;
Thou dost preserve the stars from wrong;
And the most ancient heavens, through thee, are fresh and strong.

To humbler functions, awful Power!
I call thee: I myself commend

Unto thy guidance from this hour;
Oh, let my weakness have an end!
Give unto me, made lowly wise,
The spirit of self-sacrifice;
The confidence of reason give,
And in the light of truth thy bondman let me
    live!

THE INFLUENCE OF NATURE

    These beauteous forms,
Through a long absence, have not been to me
As is a landscape to a blind man's eye;
But oft in lonely rooms, and 'mid the din
Of towns and cities, I have owed to them,
In hours of weariness, sensations sweet,
Felt in the blood, and felt along the heart;
And passing even into my purer mind
With tranquil restoration:—feelings too,
Of unremembered pleasure: such, perhaps,
As have no slight or trivial influence
On that best portion of a good man's life,
His little, nameless, unremembered acts
Of kindness and of love. Nor less I trust
To them I may have owed another gift
Of aspect more sublime; that blessed mood
In which the burthen of the mystery,
In which the heavy and the weary weight
Of all this unintelligible world,
Is lightened:—that serene and blessed mood

In which the affections gently lead us on,—
Until, the breath of this corporeal frame,
And even the motion of our human blood,
Almost suspended, we are laid asleep
In body, and become a living soul :
While with an eye made quiet by the power
Of harmony, and the deep power of joy,
We see into the life of things.

. . . . .

     I have learned
To look on nature, not as in the hour
Of thoughtless youth ; but hearing oftentimes
The still, sad music of humanity,
Nor harsh, nor grating, though of ample power
To chasten and subdue. And I have felt
A presence that disturbs me with the joy
Of elevated thoughts : a sense sublime
Of something far more deeply interfused,
Whose dwelling is the light of setting suns,
And the round ocean, and the living air,
And the blue sky, and in the mind of man :
A motion and a spirit, that impels
All thinking things, all objects of all thought,
And rolls through all things.

AN EVENING VOLUNTARY

Not in the lucid intervals of life
That come but as a curse to party strife ;
Not in some hour when Pleasure with a sigh
Of languor puts his rosy garland by ;

Not in the breathing-times of that poor slave
Who daily piles up wealth in Mammon's cave—
Is Nature felt, or can be ; nor do words,
Which practised talent readily affords,
Prove that her hand has touched responsive
    chords ;
Nor has her gentle beauty power to move
With genuine rapture and with fervent love
The soul of genius, if he dare to take
Life's rule from passion craved for passion's sake ;
Untaught that meekness is the cherished bent
Of all the truly great and all the innocent.

    But who *is* innocent ? By grace divine,
Not otherwise, O Nature, we are thine,
Through good and evil thine, in just degree
Of rational and manly sympathy.
To all that earth from pensive hearts is stealing,
And Heaven is now to gladdened eyes re-
    vealing,
Add every charm the universe can show
Through every change its aspects undergo.
Care may be respited, but not repealed ;
No perfect cure grows on that bounded field.
Vain is the pleasure, a false calm the peace,
If He, through whom alone our conflicts cease,
Our virtuous hopes without relapse advance,
Come not to speed the Soul's deliverance ;
To the distempered Intellect refuse
His gracious help, or give what we abuse.

My heart leaps up when I behold
    A rainbow in the sky:
So was it when my life began;
So is it now I am a man;
So be it when I shall grow old,
    Or let me die!
The child is father of the man;
And I could wish my days to be
Bound each to each by natural piety.

It is a beauteous evening, calm and free;
The holy time is quiet as a nun
Breathless with adoration; the broad sun
Is sinking down in its tranquillity;
The gentleness of heaven is on the sea:
Listen: the mighty Being is awake,
And doth with his eternal motion make
A sound like thunder—everlastingly.
Dear child! dear girl! that walkest with me here,
If thou appear untouched by solemn thought,
Thy nature is not therefore less divine:
Thou liest in Abraham's bosom all the year;
And worshipp'st at the temple's inner shrine,
God being with thee when we know it not.

WRITTEN IN KING'S COLLEGE CHAPEL, CAMBRIDGE

Tax not the royal saint with vain expense,
With ill-matched aims the architect who planned,
Albeit labouring for a scanty band
Of white-robed scholars only, this immense
And glorious work of fine intelligence!
Give all thou canst; high Heaven rejects the lore
Of nicely-calculated less or more;
So deemed the man who fashioned for the sense
These lofty pillars, spread that branching roof,
Self-poised, and scooped into ten thousand cells,
Where light and shade repose, where music dwells,
Lingering—and wandering on as loth to die;
Like thoughts whose very sweetness yieldeth proof
That they were born for immortality.

TRUTH AND CHANGE

Truth fails not; but her outward forms that bear
The longest date do melt like frosty rime,

That in the morning whitened hill and plain
And is no more; drop like the tower sublime
Of yesterday, which royally did wear
His crown of weeds, but could not even sustain
Some casual shout that broke the silent air,
Or the unimaginable touch of Time.

CHILDHOOD AND AGE

OUR birth is but a sleep and a forgetting;
The Soul that rises with us, our life's Star,
    Hath had elsewhere its setting,
        And cometh from afar:
    Not in entire forgetfulness
    And not in utter nakedness,
But trailing clouds of glory do we come
    From God, who is our home:
Heaven lies about us in our infancy!
Shades of the prison-house begin to close
    Upon the growing boy,
But he beholds the light, and whence it flows,
    He sees it in his joy;
The youth, who daily farther from the east
    Must travel, still is nature's priest,
    And by the vision splendid
    Is on his way attended;
At length the man perceives it die away,
And fade into the light of common day.

O joy ! that in our embers
Is something that doth live,
That nature yet remembers
What was so fugitive !
The thought of our past years in me doth breed
Perpetual benediction : not indeed
For that which is most worthy to be blest—
Delight and liberty, the simple creed
Of childhood, whether busy or at rest,
With new-fledged hope still fluttering in his breast :—
    Not for these I raise
    The song of thanks and praise ;
    But for those obstinate questionings
    Of sense and outward things,
    Fallings from us, vanishings ;
    Blank misgivings of a creature
Moving about in worlds not realised,
High instincts before which our mortal nature
Did tremble like a guilty thing surprised :
    But for those first affections,
    Those shadowy recollections,
    Which, be they what they may,
Are yet the fountain light of all our day,
Are yet a master light of all our seeing ;
Uphold us, cherish, and have power to make
Our noisy years seem moments in the being
Of the eternal silence : truths that wake,
    To perish never ;
Which neither listlessness, nor mad endeavour,

        Nor man nor boy,
      Nor all that is at enmity with joy,
Can utterly abolish or destroy!
        Hence in a season of calm weather,
        Though inland far we be,
Our souls have sight of that immortal sea
        Which brought us hither,
        Can in a moment travel thither,
And see the children sport upon the shore,
And hear the mighty waters rolling evermore.
                    William Wordsworth.

THE NATIVITY

She gave with joy her virgin breast;
She hid it not, she bared the breast
Which suckled that divinest babe!
Blessed, blessed, were the breasts
Which the Saviour infant kissed;
And blessed, blessed was the mother,
Who wrapped His limbs in swaddling clothes,
Singing placed Him on her lap,
Hung o'er Him with her looks of love,
And soothed Him with a lulling motion.
Blessed, for she sheltered Him
From the damp and chilling air;
Blessed, blessed, for she lay
With such a babe in one blest bed,
Close as babes and mothers lie.
Blessed, blessed evermore,
With her virgin lips she kiss'd,
With her arms and to her breast
She embraced the babe divine,
Her babe divine the virgin mother!
There lives not on this ring of earth
A mortal that can sing her praise.
Mighty mother, virgin pure,
In the darkness and the night,
For us she bore the heavenly Lord

TO HIS CHILD

DEAR babe, that sleepest cradled by my side,
Whose gentle breathings, heard in this deep calm,
Fill up the interspersed vacancies
And momentary pauses of the thought;
My babe so beautiful, it thrills my heart
With tender gladness thus to look at thee,
And think that thou shalt learn far other lore
And in far other scenes! For I was reared
In the great city, pent mid cloisters dim,
And saw nought lovely but the sky and stars.
But thou, my babe, shalt wander like a breeze
By lakes and sandy shores, beneath the crags
Of ancient mountain, and beneath the clouds
Which image in their bulk both lakes and shores
And mountain crags: so shalt thou see and hear
The lovely shapes and sounds intelligible
Of that eternal language, which thy God
Utters, who from eternity doth teach
Himself in all, and all things in Himself.
Great universal Teacher, He shall mould
Thy spirit, and by giving make it ask.
Therefore all seasons shall be sweet to thee,
Whether the summer clothe the general earth
With greenness, or the redbreast sit and sing
Betwixt the tufts of snow on the bare branch

Of mossy apple-tree, while the nigh thatch
Smokes in the sun-thaw; whether the eave-drops fall
Heard only in the trances of the blast,
Or if the secret ministry of frost
Shall hang them up in silent icicles,
Quietly shining to the quiet moon.

ON HIS BAPTISMAL BIRTHDAY

God's child in Christ adopted,—Christ my all—
What that earth boasts were not lost cheaply rather
Than forfeit that blest name, by which I call
The Holy One, the Almighty God, my Father?
Father! in Christ we live, and Christ in Thee,
Eternal Thou, and everlasting we.
The heir of heaven, henceforth I fear not death;
In Christ I live! in Christ I draw the breath
Of the true life! Let then earth, sea, and sky
Make war against me; on my front I show
Their mighty Master's seal. In vain they try
To end my life, that can but end its woe.
Is that a death-bed where a Christian lies?
Yes, but not his—'Tis Death itself there dies.

JOY

    My genial spirits fail;
    And what can these avail
To lift the smothering weight from off my breast?
    It were a vain endeavour,
    Though I should gaze for ever
On that green light that lingers in the west:
I may not hope from outward forms to win
The passion and the life, whose fountains are within.

O Lady! we receive but what we give,
And in our life alone does Nature live:
Ours is her wedding garment, ours her shroud!
    And would we ought behold, of higher worth,
Than that inanimate cold world allowed
To the poor loveless ever-anxious crowd,
    Ah, from the soul itself must issue forth
A light, a glory, a fair luminous cloud
      Enveloping the earth—
And from the soul itself must there be sent
    A sweet and potent voice, of its own birth,
Of all sweet sounds the life and element!

O pure of heart! thou need'st not ask of me
What this strong music in the soul may be!

What, and wherein it doth exist
This light, this glory, this fair luminous mist,
This beautiful and beauty-making power.
   Joy, virtuous Lady ! joy that ne'er was given
Save to the pure, and in their purest hour,
Life, and life's effluence, cloud at once and shower ;
Joy, Lady ! is the spirit and the power,
Which wedding Nature to us gives in dower,
   A new Earth and new Heaven,
Undreamt of by the sensual and the proud—
Joy is the sweet voice, joy the luminous cloud—
   We in ourselves rejoice !
And thence flows all that charms or ear or sight,
   All melodies the echoes of that voice,
All colours a suffusion from that light.
Samuel Taylor Coleridge.

THE JUST SHALL LIVE BY FAITH

"The just shall live by faith,"—and why?
    That faith
By which they live is all that makes them just,
The sole antagonist to the inborn lust
And malice that subjects them to the death
Which Adam earn'd, Cain, Abel suffered, Seth
Bequeath'd to all his progeny; who must
Suffer the primal doom of dust to dust,
And for uncertain respite hold their breath.
Think not the faith by which the just shall live
Is a dead creed, a map correct of heaven,
Far less a feeling fond and fugitive,
A thoughtless gift, withdrawn as soon as given.
It is an affirmation and an act
That bids eternal truth be present fact.

PRAYER

I.

There is an awful quiet in the air,
And the sad earth, with moist imploring eye,
Looks wide and wakeful at the pondering sky,
Like Patience slow subsiding to Despair.

But see, the blue smoke, as a voiceless prayer,
Sole witness of a secret sacrifice,
Unfolds its tardy wreaths, and multiplies
Its soft chameleon breathings in the rare
Capacious ether,—so it fades away,
And nought is seen beneath the pendent blue,
The undistinguishable waste of day.
So have I dreamed!—oh, may the dream be true!—
That praying souls are purged from mortal hue,
And grow as pure as He to whom they pray.

II.

Be not afraid to pray—to pray is right.
Pray, if thou canst, with hope; but ever pray,
Though hope be weak, or sick with long delay;
Pray in the darkness if there be no light.
Far is the time, remote from human sight,
When war and discord on the earth shall cease;
Yet every prayer for universal peace
Avails the blessed time to expedite.
Whate'er is good to wish, ask that of Heaven,
Though it be what thou can'st not hope to see;
Pray to be perfect, though material leaven
Forbid the Spirit so on earth to be;
But if for any wish thou darest not pray,
Then pray to God to cast that wish away.

Hartley Coleridge.

HOLY BAPTISM

O happy arms where cradled lies,
   And ready for the Lord's embrace,
     That precious sacrifice,
        The darling of His grace!

Blest eyes, that see the smiling gleam
   Upon the slumbering features glow,
     When the life-giving stream
        Touches the tender brow.

Or when the holy cross is sign'd,
   And the young soldier duly sworn,
     With true and fearless mind,
        To serve the Virgin-born.

But happiest ye, who, sealed and blest,
   Back to your arms your treasure take,
     With Jesus' mark impressed,
        To nurse for Jesus' sake.

By whom Love's daily touch is seen,
   In strengthening form and freshening hue,
     In the fix'd brow serene,
        The deep yet eager view.

O tender gem, and full of heaven !
Not in the twilight stars on high,
Not in moist flowers at even,
See we our God so nigh.

ANGELS AND CHILDREN

Heaven in the depth and height is seen,
On high among the stars, and low
In deep, clear waters ; all between
Is earth and tastes of earth : even so
The Almighty One draws near
To strongest seraphs there, to weakest infants here.

And both are robed in white, and both
On evil look unharmed, and wear
A ray so pure, ill powers are loth
To linger in the keen bright air.
As angels wait in joy
On saints, so on the old the duteous-hearted boy.

God's angels keep the eternal round
Of praise on high, and never tire ;
His lambs are in His temple found
Early, with all their heart's desire.
They boast not to be free,
They grudge not to their Lord meek ear and bended knee.

O well and wisely wrought of old,
　Nor without guide, be sure, who first
Did cherub forms as infants mould,
　And lift them where the full deep burst
　　　Of awful harmony
Might need them most, to waft it onward to the sky.

THE TWO COVENANTS

　Now of Thy love we deem
　　As of an ocean vast,
Mounting in tides against the stream
　　Of ages gone and past.

　Both theirs and ours Thou art,
　　As we and they are Thine;
Kings, prophets, patriarchs—all have part
　　Along the sacred line.

　O bond of union, dear
　　And strong as is Thy grace!
Saints, parted by a thousand year,
　　May thus in heart embrace.

THE WATERFALL

Mark how, a thousand streams in one,
  One in a thousand, on they fare;
    Now flashing to the sun,
      Now still as beast in lair.

Now round the rock, now mounting o'er,
  In lawless dance they win their way;
    Still seeming more and more
      To swell as we survey.

They win their way, and find their rest
  Together in their ocean home;
    From East and weary West,
      From North and South they come.

They rush and roar, they whirl and leap,
  Not wilder drives the wintry storm;
    Yet a strong law they keep,
      Strange powers their course inform.

Even so the mighty sky-born stream :—
  Its living waters from above
    All marred and broken seem,
      No union and no love.

Yet in dim caves they haply blend,
  In dreams of mortals unespied;
    One is their awful End,
      One their unfailing Guide.

SONG OF THE MANNA-GATHERERS

Comrades, haste! the tents' tall shading
  Lies along the level sand
Far and faint; the stars are fading
  O'er the gleaming western strand;
    Airs of morning
  Freshen the bleak burning land.

Haste, or ere the third hour glowing
  With its eager thirst prevail
O'er the moist pearls, now bestrowing
  Thymy slope and rushy vale,—
    Dews celestial,
  Left when earthly dews exhale.

Sing we thus our songs of labour
  At our harvest in the wild,
For our God and for our neighbour,
  Till six times the morn have smiled,
    And our vessels
  Are with twofold treasure piled.

Comrades, what our sires have told us—
  Watch and wait, for it will come;
Smiling vales shall soon enfold us
  In a new and vernal home;
    Earth will feed us
  From her own benignant womb.

Not by manna-showers at morning
   Shall our board be then supplied,
But a strange pale gold, adorning
   Many a tufted mountain's side,
     Yearly feed us,
   Year by year our murmurings chide,

There, no prophet's touch awaiting,
   From each cool deep cavern start
Rills, that since their first creating
   Ne'er have ceased to sing their part.
     Oft we hear them
   In our dreams, with thirsty heart.

THE VOICE OF NATURE

SIN is with man at morning break,
   And through the livelong day
Deafens the ear that fain would wake
   To Nature's simple lay.

But when eve's silent footfall steals
   Along the eastern sky,
And one by one to earth reveals
   Those purer fires on high,

When one by one each human sound
   Dies on the awful ear,
Then Nature's voice no more is drown'd,
   She speaks, and we must hear.

Then pours she on the Christian heart
    That warning still and deep,
At which high spirits of old would start
    Even from their Pagan sleep,

Just guessing, through their murky blind,
    Few, faint, and baffling sight,
Streaks of a brighter heaven behind,
    A cloudless depth of light.

PREVENIENT GRACE

Draw near as early as we may,
    Grace, like an angel, goes before;
The stone is roll'd away,
    We find an open door.

O wondrous chain! where aye entwine
    Our human wills, a tender thread,
With the strong will divine;
    We run as we are led.

We, did I say? 'tis all Thine own,
    Thou in the dark dost Mary guide;
Thine angel moves the stone,
    Love feels Thee at her side.

LONELINESS

Why should we faint and fear to live alone,
    Since all alone, so Heav'n has willed, we die;
Not e'en the tenderest heart, and next our own,
    Knows half the reasons why we smile or sigh.

Each in his hidden sphere of joy or woe,
    Our hermit spirits dwell, and range apart;
Our eyes see all around in gloom or glow,
    Hues of their own, fresh borrow'd from the heart.

SOWING AND REAPING

We scatter seeds with careless hand,
And dream we ne'er shall see them more:
    But for a thousand years
      Their fruit appears
    In weeds that mar the land,
      Or healthful store.

The deeds we do, the words we say,
Into still air they seem to fleet:
    We count them ever past,
      But they shall last.
    In the dread judgment they
      And we shall meet.

THE POWER OF PRAYER

THINK ye the spires that glow so bright,
   In front of yonder setting sun,
Stand by their own unshaken might?
   No—where th' upholding grace is won
We dare not ask, nor Heaven would tell ;
But sure from many a hidden dell,
From many a rural nook unthought of there,
Rises for that proud world the saints' prevailing prayer.

PENANCE·

How welcome, in the sweet still hour,
   Falls on the weary heart,
     Listening apart,
Each rustling note from breeze and bower ;
   The mimic rain mid poplar leaves,
   The mist-drops from the o'erloaded eaves,
   Sighs that the herd half-dreaming heaves,
Or owlet chanting his dim part ;
   Or trickling of imprison'd rill
   Heard faintly down some pastoral hill,
   His pledge, who rules the froward will
With more than kingly power, with more than wizard art.

But never mourner's ear so keen
    Watch'd for the soothing sounds
    That walk their rounds
Upon the moonlight air serene,
    As the bright sentinels on high
    Stoop to receive each contrite sigh,
    When the hot world hath hurried by,
And souls have time to feel their wounds.
    Nor ever tenderest bosom beat
    So truly to the noiseless feet
    Of shadows that from light clouds fleet,
Where Ocean gently rocks within his summer bounds,
    As saints around the Glory-Throne
    To each faint sigh respond
    And yearning fond
    Of penitents that inly moan.

THE BURIAL OF THE DEAD

The deep knell dying down, the mourners pause,
Waiting their Saviour's welcome at the gate;
    Sure with the words of Heaven
    Thy Spirit met us there,

And sought with us along the accustom'd way
The hallow'd porch, and entering in beheld
    The pageant of sad joy
    So dear to Faith and Hope.

O hadst thou brought a strain from Paradise
To cheer us, happy soul, thou hadst not touched
    The sacred springs of grief
    More tenderly and true,

Than those deep-warbled anthems, high and low,
Low as the grave, high as th' Eternal Throne;
    Guiding through light and gloom
    Our mourning fancies wild,

Till gently, like soft golden clouds at eve
Around the western twilight, all subside
    Into a placid faith,
    That even with beaming eye

Counts thy sad honours, coffin, bier, and pall,
(So many relics of a frail love lost),
    So many tokens dear
    Of endless love begun.

John Keble.

DE PROFUNDIS

O FATHER, in that hour
When Earth all succouring power
    Shall disavow ;
When spear and shield and crown
In faintness are cast down ;
    Sustain us Thou !

By Him who bowed to take
The death cup for our sake,
    The thorn, the rod ;
From whom the last dismay
Was not to pass away ;
    Aid us, O God !
Felicia Dorothea Hemans.

SEPARATION OF FRIENDS

Do not their souls, who 'neath the altar wait
   Until their second birth,
The gift of patience need, as separate
   From their first friends of earth?
Not that earth's blessings are not all outshone
   By Eden's angel flame,
But that earth knows not yet, the Dead has won
   That crown which was his aim.
For when he left it, 'twas a twilight scene
   About his silent bier,
A breathless struggle, faith and sight between,
   And Hope and sacred Fear.
Fear startled at his pains and dreary end,
   Hope raised her chalice high,
And the twin-sisters still his shade attend,
   View'd in the mourner's eye.
So day by day for him from earth ascends,
   As steam in summer even,
The speechless intercession of his friends,
   Toward the azure heaven.

Ah ! dearest, with a word he could dispel
   All questioning, and raise
Our hearts to rapture, whispering all was
    well,
   And turning prayer to praise.
And other secrets too he could declare,
   By patterns all divine,
His earthly creed retouching here and there,
   And deepening every line.
Dearest ! he longs to speak, as I to know,
   And yet we both refrain :
It were not good : a little doubt below,
   And all will soon be plain.

A VOICE FROM AFAR

     WEEP not for me :—
Be blithe as wont, nor tinge with gloom
The stream of love that circles home,
     Light hearts and free !
Joy in the gifts Heaven's bounty lends ;
   Nor miss my face, dear friends !

     I still am near ;—
Watching the smiles I prized on earth,
Your converse mild, your blameless mirth ;
     Now too I hear
Of whisper'd sounds the tale complete,
   Low prayers, and musings sweet.

   A sea before
The Throne is spread :—its pure still glass
Pictures all earth-scenes as they pass.
   We, on its shore,
Share, in the bosom of our rest,
  God's knowledge, and are blest.

WAITING FOR THE MORNING

   THEY are at rest:
We may not stir the heaven of their repose
With loud-voiced grief, or passionate request,
   Or selfish plaint for those
Who in the mountain grots of Eden lie,
And hear the fourfold river as it hurries by.

   They hear it sweep
In distance down the dark and savage vale;
But they at eddying pool or current deep
   Shall never more grow pale;
They hear, and meekly muse, as fain to know
How long untired, unspent, that giant stream shall flow.

   And soothing sounds
Blend with the neighbouring waters as they glide;

Posted along the haunted garden's bounds
    Angelic forms abide,
Echoing as words of watch, o'er lawn and grove,
The verses of that hymn which seraphs chant above.

Cardinal Newman.

When up to nightly skies we gaze,
Where stars pursue their endless ways,
We think we see from earth's low clod
The wide and shining home of God.

But could we rise to moon or sun,
Or path where planets duly run,
Still heaven would spread above us far,
And earth remote would seem a star.

This earth with all its dust and tears
Is His no less than yonder spheres;
And raindrops weak, and grains of sand,
Are stamped by His immediate hand.

The rock, the wave, the little flower,—
All fed by streams of living power
That spring from one almighty will,—
Whate'er His thought conceives fulfil.

We view those halls of painted air,
And own Thy presence makes them fair;
But nearer still to Thee, O Lord,
Is he whose thoughts with Thine accord.

John Sterling.

THE KINGDOM OF GOD

I say to thee, do thou repeat
To the first man thou mayest meet
In lane, highway, or open street—

That he and we and all men move
Under a canopy of love,
As broad as the blue sky above;

That doubt and trouble, fear and pain
And anguish, all are shadows vain,
That death itself shall not remain;

That weary deserts we may tread,
A dreary labyrinth may thread,
Through dark ways underground be led;

Yet, if we will one Guide obey,
The dreariest path, the darkest way,
Shall issue out in heavenly day.

And we, on divers shores now cast,
Shall meet, our perilous voyage past,
All in our Father's house at last.

And ere thou leave him, say thou this
Yet one word more—they only miss
The winning of that final bliss,

Who will not count it true that Love,
Blessing, not cursing, rules above,
And that in it we live and move.

And one thing further make him know,
That to believe these things are so,
This firm faith never to forego,

Despite of all which seems at strife
With blessings, all with curses rife,
That this *is* blessing, this *is* life.

Not Thou from us, O Lord, but we
Withdraw ourselves from Thee.

When we are dark and dead,
And Thou art covered with a cloud
Hanging before Thee, like a shroud,
So that our prayer can find no way,
Oh! teach us that we do not say,
"Where is *Thy* brightness fled?"

But that we search and try
What in ourselves has wrought this blame,
For Thou remainest still the same,
But earth's own vapours earth may fill
With darkness and thick clouds, while still
The sun is in the sky.

LORD, many times I am aweary quite
　　Of mine own self, my sin, my vanity—
Yet be not Thou, or I am lost outright,
　　　　Weary of me.

And hate against myself I often bear,
　　And enter with myself in fierce debate :
Take Thou my part against myself, nor share
　　　　In that just hate.

Best friends might loathe us, if what things perverse
　　We know of our own selves, they also knew :
Lord, Holy One ! if Thou who knowest worse
　　　　Shouldst loathe us too !

　　A GENIAL moment oft has given
　　　　What years of toil and pain,
　　Of long industrious toil, have striven
　　　　To win, and all in vain.

　　Yet count not, when thine end is won,
　　　　That labour merely lost ;
　　Nor say it had been wiser done
　　　　To spare the painful cost.

When heaped upon the altar lie
  All things to feed the fire—
One spark alighting from on high,
  The flames at once aspire;

But those sweet gums and fragrant woods,
  Its rich materials rare,
By tedious quest o'er lands and floods
  Had first been gathered there.

LINES

WRITTEN AFTER HEARING SOME BEAUTIFUL SINGING IN A CONVENT CHURCH AT ROME

Sweet voices! seldom mortal ear
Strains of such potency might hear;
My soul that listened seemed quite gone,
Dissolved in sweetness, and anon
I was borne upward, till I trod
Among the hierarchy of God.
And when they ceased, as time must bring
An end to every sweetest thing,
With what reluctancy came back
My spirits to their wonted track,
And how I loathed the common life,
The daily and recurring strife
With petty sins, the lowly road,
And being's ordinary load.

— Why, after such a solemn mood,
Should any meaner thought intrude?
Why will not heaven hereafter give,
That we for evermore may live
Thus at our spirit's topmost bent?
So asked I in my discontent.

But give me, Lord, a wiser heart;
These seasons come, and they depart,
These seasons, and those higher still,
When we are given to have our fill
Of strength and life and joy with Thee,
And brightness of Thy face to see.
They come, or we could never guess
Of heaven's sublimer blessedness;
They come, to be our strength and cheer
In other times, in doubt or fear,
Or should our solitary way
Lie through the desert many a day.
They go, they leave us blank and dead,
That we may learn, when they are fled,
We are but vapours which have won
A moment's brightness from the sun,
And which it may at pleasure fill
With splendour, or unclothe at will.
Well for us they do not abide,
Or we should lose ourselves in pride,
And be as angels—but as they
Who on the battlements of day
Walked, gazing on their power and might,
Till they grew giddy in their height.

Then welcome every nobler time,
When out of reach of earth's dull chime
'Tis ours to drink with purgèd ears
The music of the solemn spheres,
Or in the desert to have sight
Of those enchanted cities bright,
Which sensual eye can never see:
Thrice welcome may such seasons be:
But welcome too the common way,
The lowly duties of the day,
And all which makes and keeps us low,
Which teaches us ourselves to know,
That we who do our lineage high
Draw from beyond the starry sky,
Are yet upon the other side
To earth and to its dust allied.

THE HOLY EUCHARIST

Honey in the lion's mouth,
Emblem mystical, divine,
How the sweet and strong combine;
Cloven rock for Israel's drouth;
Treasure-house of golden grain,
By our Joseph laid in store,
In his brethren's famine sore
Freely to dispense again;
Dew on Gideon's snowy fleece;
Well from bitter changed to sweet;

Shew-bread laid in order meet,
Bread whose cost doth not increase
Though no rain in April fall ;
Horeb's manna, freely given,
Showered in white dew from heaven,
Marvellous, angelical ;
Weightiest bunch of Canaan's vine ;
Cake to strengthen and sustain
Through long days of desert pain ;
Salem's Monarch's bread and wine ;—
Thou the antidote shalt be
Of my sickness and my sin,
Consolation, medicine,
Life and Sacrament to me.

PRAYER

When prayer delights thee least, then learn to say,
Soul, now is greatest need that thou shouldst pray.

Crookèd and warped I am, and I would fain
Straighten myself by thy right line again.

O come, warm sun, and ripen my late fruits ;
Pierce, genial showers, down to my parched roots.

My well is bitter; cast therein the tree,
That sweet henceforth its brackish waves may be.

Say, what is prayer, when it is prayer indeed?
The mighty utterance of a mighty need.

The man is praying, who doth press with might
Out of his darkness into God's own light.

White heat the iron in the furnace won;
Withdrawn from thence, 'tis cold and hard anon.

Flowers from their stalks divided, presently
Droop, fail, and wither in the gazer's eye.

The greenest leaf divided from its stem
To speedy withering doth itself condemn.

The largest river from its fountain head
Cut off, leaves soon a parched and dusty bed.

All things that live from God their sustenance wait,
And sun and moon are beggars at His gate.

All skirts extended of thy mantle hold,
When angel-hands from heaven are scattering gold.

COUPLETS

To halls of heavenly truth admission wouldst thou win,
Oft Knowledge stands without, while Love may enter in.

Who praises God the most, what says he more than he
Who silent is? Yet who would therefore silent be?

From our ill-ordered hearts we oft are fain to roam,
As men go forth who find unquietness at home.

Before the eyes of men let duly shine thy light,
But ever let thy life's best part be out of sight.

My proud foe at my hands to take no boon will choose—
Thy prayers are that one gift which he cannot refuse.

Wouldst thou go forth to bless, be sure of thine own ground;
Fix well thy centre first, then draw thy circles round.

The man is happy, Lord, who love like this doth owe,
Loves Thee, his friend in Thee, and for Thy sake his foe.

Why win we not at once what we in prayer require?
That we may learn great things as greatly to desire.

The tasks, the joys of earth, the same in heaven will be;
Only the little brook has widened to a sea.

Archbishop Trench.

HEAVEN AND EARTH

God, who with thunders and great voices kept
Beneath Thy throne, and stars most silver-paced
Along the inferior gyres, and open-faced
Melodious angels round,—canst intercept
Music with music,—yet, at will, has swept
All back, all back, (said he in Patmos placed)
To fill the heavens with silence of the waste
Which lasted half an hour! Lo, I who have wept
All day and night, beseech Thee by my tears,
And by that dread response of curse and groan
Men alternate across these hemispheres,
Vouchsafe us such a half hour's hush alone,
In compensation for our stormy years!
As heaven has paused from song, let earth from moan.

WORK

What are we set on earth for? Say, to toil;
Nor seek to leave thy tending of the vines,
For all the heat o' the day, till it declines,
And Death's wild curfew shall from work assoil.

God did anoint thee with His odorous oil
To wrestle, not to reign ; and He assigns
All thy tears over, like pure crystallines,
For younger fellow-workers of the soil
To wear for amulets. So others shall
Take patience, labour, to their heart and hand,
From thy hand and thy heart and thy brave
    cheer ;
And God's grace fructify through thee to all.
The least flower with a brimming cup may stand
And share its dewdrop with another near.

BEREAVEMENT

When some belovèds, 'neath whose eyelids lay
The sweet lights of my childhood, one by one
Did leave me dark before the natural sun,
And I astonied fell and could not pray,
A thought within me to myself did say,
" Is God less God, that *thou* art left undone ?
Rise, worship, bless Him, in this sackcloth
    spun,
As in that purple ! " But I answered, Nay !
What child his filial heart in words can loose,
If he behold his tender father raise
The hand that chastens sorely ? Can he choose
But sob in silence with an upward gaze ?
And my great Father, thinking fit to bruise,
Discerns in speechless tears both prayer and
    praise.

SUBSTITUTION

When some belovèd voice that was to you
Both sound and sweetness, faileth suddenly,
And silence against which you dare not cry
Aches round you like a strong disease and new—
What hope ? what help ? what music will undo
That silence to your sense ?   Not friendship's sigh,
Not reason's subtle count ; not melody
Of viols, nor of pipes that Faunus blew ;
Not songs of poets, nor of nightingales,
Whose hearts leap upward through the cypress trees
To the clear moon ! nor yet the spheric laws
Self-chanted, nor the angels' sweet All hails,
Met in the smile of God.   Nay, none of these.
Speak Thou, availing Christ ! and fill this pause.

THE PROSPECT

Methinks we do as fretful children do,
Leaning their faces on the window-pane
To sigh the glass dim with their own breath's stain,
And shut the sky and landscape from their view
And thus, alas ! since God the Maker drew
A mystic separation 'twixt those twain,
The life beyond us, and our souls in pain,

We miss the prospect which we are called unto,
By grief we are fools to use.   Be still and strong,
O man, my brother, hold thy sobbing breath,
And keep thy soul's large window pure from wrong,
That so, as life's appointment issueth,
Thy vision may be clear to watch along
The sunset consummation-lights of death.
Elizabeth Barrett Browning.

SUNDAY

Though heaven's above and earth's below,
   Yet are they but one state,
And each the other with sweet skill
   Doth interpenetrate.

Yea, many a tie and office blest,
   In earthly lots uneven,
Hath an immortal place to fill,
   And is the root of heaven.

And surely Sundays bright and calm,
   So calm, so bright as this,
Are tastes imparted from above
   Of higher Sabbath bliss.

We own no gloomy ordinance,
   No weary Jewish day,
But weekly Easters, ever bright
   With pure domestic ray;

A feast of thought, a feast of sight,
   A feast of joyous sound,
A feast of thankful hearts, at rest,
   From labour's wheel unbound;

A day of such homekeeping bliss
    As on the poor may wait,
With all such lower joys as best
    Befit his human state.

He sees among the hornbeam boughs
    The little sparkling flood ;
The mill-wheel rests, a quiet thing
    Of black and mossy wood.

He sees the fields lie in the sun,
    He hears the plovers crying ;
The plough and harrow, both upturned,
    Are in the furrows lying.

In simple faith, he may believe
    That earth's diurnal way
Doth, like its blessèd Maker, pause
    Upon this hallowed day.

And should he ask, the happy man !
    If heaven be aught like this ;—
'Tis heaven within him, breeding there
    The love of quiet bliss.

Oh leave the man, my fretful friend !
    To follow Nature's ways,
Nor breathe to him that Christian feasts
    Are no true holy days.

Is earth to be as nothing here,
    When we are sons of earth ?
May not the body and the heart
    Share in the spirit's mirth ?

When thou hast cut each earthly hold
   Whereto his soul may cling,
Will the poor creature left behind
   Be more a heavenly thing?

Heaven fades away before our eyes,
   Heaven fades within our heart,
Because in thought our heaven and earth
   Are cast too far apart.

LOW SPIRITS

FEVER and fret and aimless stir
   And disappointed strife,
All chafing unsuccessful things,
   Make up the sum of life.

Love adds anxiety to toil
   And sameness doubles cares,
While one unbroken chain of work
   The flagging temper wears.

Sweet thought of God! now do thy work
   As thou hast done before;
Wake up, and tears will wake with thee,
   And the dull mood be o'er.

The very thinking of the thought,
   Without or praise or prayer,
Gives light to know, and life to do,
   And marvellous strength to bear.

THE AGONY

O Soul of Jesus, sick to death!
Thy blood and prayer together plead;
My sins have bowed Thee to the ground,
As the storm bows the feeble reed.

Midnight—and still the oppressive load
Upon Thy tortured heart doth lie;
Still the abhorred procession winds
Before Thy spirit's quailing eye.

Deep waters have come in, O Lord!
All darkly on Thy human soul;
And clouds of supernatural gloom
Around Thee are allowed to roll.

The weight of the eternal wrath
Drives over Thee with pressure dread;
And, forced upon the olive roots,
In deathlike sadness droops Thy head.

Thy spirit weighs the sins of men;
Thy science fathoms all their guilt;
Thou sickenest heavily at Thy heart,
And the pores open,—blood is spilt.

And Thou hast struggled with it, Lord!
Even to the limit of Thy strength,
While hours, whose minutes were as years,
Slowly fulfilled their weary length.

And Thou hast shuddered at each act,
And shrunk with an astonished fear,
As if Thou couldst not bear to see
The loathsomeness of sin so near.

Sin and the Father's anger! they
Have made Thy lower nature faint;
All, save the love within Thy heart,
Seemed for the moment to be spent.

My God! my God! and can it be
That I should sin so lightly now,
And think no more of evil thoughts,
Than of the wind that waves the bough?

I sin,—and heaven and earth go round,
As if no dreadful deed were done,
As if Christ's blood had never flowed
To hinder sin, or to atone.

I walk the earth with lightsome step,
Smile at the sunshine, breathe the air,
Do my own will, nor ever heed
Gethsemane and Thy long prayer.

Shall it be always thus, O Lord?
Wilt Thou not work this hour in me
The grace Thy passion merited,
Hatred of self and love of Thee?

Ever when tempted, make me see,
Beneath the olive's moon-pierced shade,
My God, alone, outstretched, and bruised,
And bleeding, on the earth He made.

And make me feel it was my sin,
As though no other sins there were,
That was to Him who bears the world
A load that He could scarcely bear!

THE SORROWFUL WORLD

I HEARD the wild beasts in the woods complain;
Some slept, while others wakened to sustain
Through night and day the sad monotonous round,
Half savage and half pitiful the sound.

The outcry rose to God through all the air,
The worship of distress, an animal prayer,
Loud vehement pleadings, not unlike to those
Job uttered in his agony of woes.

The very pauses, when they came, were rife
With sickening sounds of too successful strife,
As, when the clash of battle dies away,
The groans of night succeed the shrieks of day.

Man's scent the untamed creatures scarce can
    bear,
As if his tainted blood defiled the air ;
In the vast woods they fret as in a cage,
Or fly in fear, or gnash their teeth with rage.

The beasts of burden linger on their way,
Like slaves who will not speak when they obey ;
Their faces, when their looks to us they raise,
With something of reproachful patience gaze.

All creatures round us seem to disapprove ;
Their eyes discomfort us with lack of love ;
Our very rights, with signs like these alloyed,
Not without sad misgivings are enjoyed.

Earth seems to make a sound in places lone,
Sleeps through the day, but wakes at night to
    moan,
Shunning our confidence, as if we were
A guilty burden it could hardly bear.

The winds can never sing but they must wail ;
Waters lift up sad voices in the vale ;
One mountain-hollow to another calls
With broken cries of plaining waterfalls.

Silence itself is but a heaviness,
As if the earth were fainting in distress,
Like one who wakes at night in panic fears,
And nought but his own beating pulses hears.

Inanimate things can rise into despair;
And, when the thunders bellow in the air
Amid the mountains, Earth sends forth a cry
Like dying monsters in their agony.

The sea, unmated creature, tired and lone,
Makes on its desolate sands eternal moan:
Lakes on the calmest days are ever throbbing
Upon their pebbly shores with petulant sobbing.

O'er the white waste, cold grimly overawes
And hushes life beneath its merciless laws;
Invisible heat drops down from tropic skies,
And o'er the land, like an oppression, lies.

The clouds in heaven their placid motions borrow
From the funereal tread of men in sorrow;
Or, when they scud across the stormy day,
Mimic the flight of hosts in disarray.

Mostly men's many-featured faces wear
Looks of fixed gloom, or else of restless care;
The very babes, that in their cradles lie,
Out of the depths of unknown troubles cry.

Labour itself is but a sorrowful song,
The protest of the weak against the strong;
Over rough waters, and in obstinate fields,
And from dank mines, the same sad sound it yields.

O God! the fountain of perennial gladness!
Thy whole creation overflows with sadness;
Sights, sounds, are full of sorrow and alarm;
Even sweet scents have but a pensive charm.

Doth Earth send nothing up to Thee but moans?
Father! canst Thou find melody in groans?
Oh can it be, that Thou, the God of bliss,
Canst feed Thy glory on a world like this?

Ah me! that sin should have such chemic power
To turn to dross the gold of Nature's dower,
And straightway, of its single self, unbind
The eternal vision of Thy jubilant mind!

Alas! of all this sorrow there is need;
For us Earth weeps, for us the creatures bleed:
Thou art content, if all this woe imparts
The sense of exile to repentant hearts.

Yes! it is well for us: from these alarms,
Like children scared we fly into Thine arms;
And pressing sorrows put our pride to rout
With a swift faith which has not time to doubt.

We cannot herd in peace with wild beasts rude;
We dare not live in Nature's solitude;
In how few eyes of men can we behold
Enough of love to make us calm and bold?

Oh, it is well for us : with angry glance
Life glares at us, or looks at us askance :
Seek where we will,—Father ! we see it now,—
None love us, trust us, welcome us, but Thou.
Frederick William Faber.

HALLELUJAH!

Lord, all things everywhere
Thy mighty praise declare;
Some may muse, and some may sing,
But they all are worshipping:
Or by silence or by sound
Thou art praised the world around.

Ever the circling earth
Gives night and morning birth;
Every moment some place knows
Work returning or repose;
Some things wake, and some things rest;
But by all Thy love is blest.

The stormy seas and calm
Join in a giant psalm,
Solemn praises unto Thee
Sounding forth unceasingly:
Verses loud and verses low
Equally Thy glory show.

The rooted mountains grand
All reverently stand,
And by silent awe express
Lowly-hearted loftiness;

Sometimes veiled, and sometimes bare,
Now for praises, now for prayer.

How doth the ample sky
Shine with Thy majesty!
Sun and stars in every clime
Keep their course and change their time;
And by sunshine or by shower
Thou art honoured every hour.

Still with unchanging plan
Thou blessest wayward man,
And the varying hours prove
That Thou hast unvarying love:
Sometimes grieved and sometimes gay,
We would trust Thee every day.

Lord, shall sin work Thee shame,
To cloud Thy glorious name!
No, Thou art so good and just,
Sin and sorrow serve Thee must:
While they last and when they die
Thou art hope, Thou victory.

The cross and sepulchre
On love the crown confer;
Suffering has vanquished pain;
Dying has made death a gain:
Wicked hands but wrought their deed,
That a Saviour might succeed.

STARS

SEE! through the heavenly arch
With silent stately march
   The starry ranks for ever sweep;
In graduate scale of might
They all are sons of light,
   And all their times and orders keep.

O glorious, countless host,
Which shall I praise the most,
   Your lustrous groups, or course exact?
Ye on your way sublime
Defy confusing time
   Your light to dim, your path distract.

Earth's early fathers saw
The gospel and the law
   In the firm beauty of the skies:
O Thou unswerving Will,
The unveiled heavens still
   Show Thee as glorious, good, and wise.

Lord of the starry night,
With awe and with delight
   Under Thy temple dome we pray:
Still as we gaze above,
Temper our fear with love,
   That we may filial homage pay.

Not as the primal force
Impelling Nature's course,
   We know Thee, but as Father dear:
Oh, if with foolish mind
We judge Thee weakly kind,
   Correct false love with filial fear.

PRAYER

I GIVE myself to prayer;
   Lord, give Thyself to me,
And let the time of my request
   Thy time of answer be.

My thoughts are like the reeds,
   And tremble as they grow,
In the sad current of a life
   That darkly runs and slow.

No song is in the air,
   But one pervading fear;
Death's shadow dims my light, and Death
   Himself is lurking near.

I am as if asleep,
   Yet conscious that I dream;
Like one who vainly strives to wake
   And free himself, I seem.

The loud distressful cry
  With which I call on Thee,
Shall wake me, Lord, to find that Thou
  Canst give me liberty.

Oh, break this darksome spell,
  This murky sadness strange,
Let me the terrors of the night
  For cheerful day exchange.

Freshen the air with wind,
  Comfort my heart with song;
Let thoughts be lilies pure, and life
  A river bright and strong.

Save me from subtle Death,
  Who, serpent-like, by fear
Palsies me for escape, yet draws
  His trembling victim near.

I give myself to prayer;
  Lord, give Thyself to me;
And in the time of my distress,
  Oh, haste and succour me.

INCONSTANCY

OH, were I ever what I am sometimes,
   And never more what I sometimes have been;
For oft my spirit, singing as it climbs,
   Can make of winter bleak a summer green:
And yet sometimes, and in the sunniest weather,
My work and I have fallen out together.

Now, earth seems drossy, heaven the land of gold,
   Anon heaven fabulous, substantial earth;
And sometimes in my God I can be bold,
   And say, " What hopes are mine in right of birth ? "
And yet sometimes at former faith I wonder,
And fears I once defied I now sink under.

Lord, rid me of this natural waywardness,
   Unworthy one who is a child of thine;
Calm let me be when rudest winds distress,
   Nor lose occasion if the day be fine;
But faithful to the light of sacred reason,
One heart be mine in every changing season.

Thomas Toke Lynch.

A NUN'S SONG

FAR among the lonely hills,
As I lay beside my sheep,
Rest came down upon my soul
From the everlasting deep.

Changeless march the stars above,
Changeless morn succeeds to even;
And the everlasting hills
Changeless watch the changeless heaven.

See the rivers how they run
Changeless to the changeless sea;
All around is forethought sure,
Fixed will and stern decree.

Can the sailor move the main?
Will the potter heed the clay?
Mortal, where the spirit drives
Thither must the wheels obey.

Neither ask, nor fret, nor strive;
Where thy path is thou shalt go.
He who made the streams of time
Wafts thee down to weal or woe.

A MOTHER'S SONG

Deep in the warm vale the village is sleeping,
Sleeping the firs on the bleak rock above;
Nought wakes save grateful hearts, silently creeping
Up to the Lord in the might of their love.

What Thou hast given to me, Lord, here I bring Thee,
Odour and light and the magic of gold;
Feet which must follow Thee, lips which must sing Thee,
Limbs which must ache for Thee ere they grow old.

What Thou hast given to me, Lord, here I tender,
Life of mine own life, the fruit of my love;
Take him, yet leave him me, till I shall render
Count of the precious charge, kneeling above.

Charles Kingsley.

"Old things need not be therefore true,"
O brother men, nor yet the new;
Ah! still awhile the old thought retain,
And yet consider it again.

The souls of now two thousand years
Have laid up here their toils and fears,
And all the earnings of their pain,—
Ah, yet consider it again!

We! what do we see? each a space
Of some few yards before his face;
Does that the whole wide plan explain?
Ah, yet consider it again!

Say not, the struggle nought availeth,
   The labour and the wounds are vain;
The enemy faints not nor faileth,
   And as things have been they remain.

If hopes were dupes, fears may be liars;
   It may be, in yon smoke concealed,
Your comrades chase e'en now the fliers,
   And, but for you, possess the field.

For while the tired waves vainly breaking
    Seem here no painful inch to gain,
Far back, through creeks and inlets making,
    Comes silent flooding in the main.

And not by eastern windows only,
    When daylight comes, comes in the light,
In front the sun climbs slow, how slowly,
    But westward, look, the land is bright.

Where lies the land to which the ship would go?
Far, far ahead, is all her seamen know.
And where the land she travels from? Away,
Far, far behind, is all that they can say.

On sunny noons upon the deck's smooth face,
Linked arm in arm, how pleasant here to pace;
Or, o'er the stern reclining, watch below
The foaming wake far-widening as we go.

On stormy nights, when wild north-westers rave,
How proud a thing to fight with wind and wave!
The dripping sailor on the reeling mast
Exults to bear, and scorns to wish it past.

Where lies the land to which the ship would go?
Far, far ahead, is all her seamen know.
And where the land she travels from? Away,
Far, far behind, is all that they can say.
                  Arthur Hugh Clough.

DESIRE

Thou, who dost dwell alone,
Thou, who dost know Thine own,
Thou, to whom all are known
From the cradle to the grave,
 Save, oh, save.
From the world's temptations,
 From tribulations;
From that fierce anguish
Wherein we languish;
From that torpor deep
Wherein we lie asleep,
Heavy as death, cold as the grave;
 Save, oh, save.

When the Soul, growing clearer,
 Sees God no nearer:
When the Soul, mounting higher,
 To God comes no nigher:
But the arch-fiend Pride
Mounts at her side,
Foiling her high emprise,
Sealing her eagle eyes,
And, when she fain would soar,
Makes idols to adore;

Changing the pure emotion
Of her high devotion
To a skin-deep sense
Of her own eloquence :
Strong to deceive, strong to enslave,
    Save, oh, save.

  From the ingrain'd fashion
Of this earthly nature
That mars thy creature.
From grief, that is but passion,
From mirth, that is but feigning ;
From tears, that bring no healing ;
From wild and weak complaining ;
  Thine old strength revealing,
    Save, oh, save.

From doubt, where all is double :
Where wise men are not strong ;
Where comfort turns to trouble,
Where just men suffer wrong ;
Where sorrow treads on joy :
Where sweet things soonest cloy :
Where faiths are built on dust :
Where love is half mistrust,
Hungry, and barren, and sharp as the sea ;
    Oh, set us free.

O let the false dream fly
Where our sick souls do lie
  Tossing continually.

O where thy voice doth come
   Let all doubts be dumb :
   Let all words be mild :
   All strifes be reconciled :
   All pains beguil'd !
Light bring no blindness ;
Love no unkindness ;
Knowledge no ruin ;
Fear no undoing.
  From the cradle to the grave,
     Save, oh, save.

MORALITY

We cannot kindle when we will
The fire which in the heart resides :
The spirit bloweth and is still,
In mystery our soul abides.
   But tasks in hours of insight will'd
   Can be through hours of gloom fulfill'd.

With aching hands and bleeding feet
We dig and heap, lay stone on stone ;
We bear the burden and the heat
Of the long day, and wish t'were done.
   Not till the hours of light return,
   All we have built do we discern.

Then when the clouds are off the soul,
When thou dost bask in Nature's eye,

Ask, how *she* view'd thy self-control,
Thy struggling task'd morality;
    Nature, whose free, light, cheerful air
    Oft made thee, in thy gloom, despair.

And she, whose censure thou dost dread,
Whose eye thou wast afraid to seek,
See, on her face a glow is spread,
A strong emotion on her cheek!
    "Ah, child!" she cries, "that strife divine,
    Whence was it, for it is not mine.

"There is no effort on *my* brow,
I do not strive, I do not weep;
I rush with the swift spheres and glow
In joy, and when I will, I sleep.
    Yet that severe, that earnest air,
    I saw, I felt it once—but where?

"I knew not yet the gauge of time,
Nor wore the manacles of space;
I felt it in some other clime,
I saw it in some other place.
    'Twas when the heavenly house I trod,
    And lay upon the breast of God."

Matthew Arnold.

AN EASTER HYMN

Awake, thou wintry earth,
  Fling off thy sadness;
Fair vernal flowers laugh forth
  Your ancient gladness:
      Christ is risen.

Wave, woods, your blossoms all,
  Grim Death is dead;
Ye weeping funeral trees,
  Lift up your head.
      Christ is risen.

Come, see, the graves are green;
  It is light; let us go
Where our loved ones rest
  In hope below.
      Christ is risen.

All is fresh and new,
  Full of spring and light;
Wintry heart, why wearest the hue
  Of sleep and night?
      Christ is risen.

Leave thy cares beneath,
  Leave thy worldly love;
Begin the better life
  With God above.
    Christ is risen.
          Thomas Blackburne.

MAGNA EST VERITAS

Here in this little bay,
Full of tumultuous life and great repose,
Where twice a day,
The purposeless glad ocean comes and goes,
Under high cliffs, and far from the huge town,
I sit me down.
For want of me the world's course will not fail;
When all its work is done, the lie shall rot;
The truth is great and shall prevail,
When none cares whether it prevail or not.

REMEMBERED GRACE

Since succour to the feeblest of the wise
Is charge of nobler weight
Than the security
Of many and many a foolish soul's estate,
This I affirm,
Though fools will fools more confidently be:
Whom God does once with heart to heart
    befriend,
He does so to the end:

And having planted Life's miraculous germ,
One sweet pulsation of responsive love,
He sets him sheer above,
Not sin and bitter shame
And wreck of fame,
But Hell's insidious and more black attempt,
The envy, malice, and pride,
Which men who share so easily condone
That few ev'n list such ills as these to hide.
From these unalterably exempt,
Through the remembered grace
Of that divine embrace,
Of his sad errors none,
Though gross to blame,
Shall cast him lower than the cleansing flame,
Nor make him quite depart
From the small flock named "after God's own heart,"
And to themselves unknown.
Nor can he quail
In faith, nor flush nor pale
When all the other idiot people spell
How this or that new prophet's word belies
Their last high oracle;
But constantly his soul
Points to its pole
Ev'n as the needle points, and knows not why;
And, under the ever-changing clouds of doubt,
When others cry,
"The stars, if stars there were,
Are quench'd and out!"

To him, uplooking t'ward the hills for aid,
Appear, at need displayed,
Gaps in the low-hung gloom, and bright in air,
Orion or the Bear.

VICTORY IN DEFEAT

  Ah, God, alas,
How soon it came to pass
The sweetness melted from Thy barbed hook
Which I so simply took;
And I lay bleeding on the bitter land,
Afraid to stir against Thy least command,
But losing all my pleasant life-blood, whence
Force should have been heart's frailty to withstand.
Life is not life at all without delight,
Nor has it any might;
And better than the insentient heart and brain
Is sharpest pain;
And better for the moment seems it to rebel,
If the great Master, from His lifted seat,
Ne'er whispers to the wearied servant "Well!"
Yet what returns of love did I endure,
When to be pardon'd seem'd almost more sweet
Than aye to have been pure!
But day still faded to disastrous night,
And thicker darkness changed to feebler light,

Until forgiveness, without stint renew'd,
Was now no more with loving tears imbued,
Vowing no more offence.
Not less to thine unfaithful didst Thou cry,
"Come back, poor child; be all as 'twas before."
But I,
"No, no: I will not promise any more!
Yet, when I feel my hour is come to die,
And so I am secured of continence,
Then may I say, though haply then in vain,
'My only, only love, O take me back again.'"
Thereafter didst Thou smite
So hard that, for a space,
Uplifted seem'd heav'n's everlasting door,
And I indeed the darling of Thy grace.
But in some dozen changes of the moon
A bitter mockery seem'd thy bitter boon.
The broken pinion was no longer sore.
Again, indeed, I woke
Under so dread a stroke
That all the strength it left within my heart
Was just to ache and turn, and then to turn and ache
And some weak sign of war unceasingly to make.
And here I lie,
With no one near to mark,
Thrusting Hell's phantoms feebly in the dark,
And still at point more utterly to die.

O God, how long!
Put forth indeed Thy powerful right hand,
While time is yet,
Or never shall I see the blissful land!
Thus I: then God, in pleasant speech and
    strong,
(Which soon I shall forget):
"The man who, though his fights be all
    defeats,
Still fights,
Enters at last
The heavenly Jerusalem's rejoicing streets
With glory more, and more triumphant rites,
Than always-conquering Joshua's, when his
    blast
The frighted walls of Jericho down cast;
And lo! the glad surprise
Of peace beyond surmise,
More than in common saints, for ever in his
    eyes."

THE TOYS

My little son, who look'd from thoughtful eyes,
And moved and spoke in quiet grown-up wise,
Having my law the seventh time disobey'd,
I struck him, and dismiss'd
With hard words and unkiss'd;

His mother, who was patient, being dead.
Then fearing lest his grief should hinder sleep,
I visited his bed,
But found him slumbering deep,
With darken'd eyelids, and their lashes yet
From his late sobbing wet.
And I with moan,
Kissing away his tears, left others of my own;
For, on a table drawn beside his head,
He had put, within his reach,
A box of counters, and a red-vein'd stone,
A piece of glass abraded by the beach,
And six or seven shells,
A bottle with bluebells,
And two French copper coins, ranged there with careful art,
To comfort his sad heart.

So when that night I pray'd
To God, I wept, and said:—
Ah, when at last we lie with trancèd breath,
Not vexing Thee in death,
And thou rememberest of what toys
We made our joys,
How weakly understood
Thy great commanded good,
Then Fatherly not less
Than I whom Thou hast moulded from the clay,
Thou'lt leave Thy wrath and say,
"I will be sorry for their childishness."

"LET BE!"

Ah, yes; we tell the good and evil trees
By fruits: But how tell these?
Who does not know
That good and ill
Are done in secret still,
And that which shows is verily but show!
How high of heart is one, and one how sweet of mood;
But not all height is holiness,
Nor every sweetness good;
And grace will sometimes lurk where who could guess?
The Critic of his kind
Dealing to each his share,
With easy humour, hard to bear,
May not impossibly have in him shrined
As in a gossamer globe or thickly padded pod,
Some small seed dear to God.
Haply yon wretch, so famous for his falls,
Got them beneath the devil-defended walls
Of some high virtue he had vow'd to win;
And that which you and I
Call his besetting sin
Is but the fume of his peculiar fire
Of inmost contrary desire,
And means wild willingness for her to die,
Dash'd with despondence of her favour sweet;
He fiercer fighting, in his worst defeat,

Than I or you,
That only courteous greet
Where he does hotly woo,
Did ever fight, in our best victory.
Another is mistook
Through his deceitful likeness to his look !
Let be, let be ;
Why should I clear myself, why answer thou
    for me ?
That shaft of slander shot
Miss'd·only the right blot.
I see the shame
They cannot see :
'Tis very just they blame
The thing that's not.

Coventry Patmore.

LONGING

O ALL wide places, far from feverous towns;
   Great shining seas; pine forests; mountains wild;
Rock-bosomed shores; rough heaths, and sheep-cropt downs;
   Vast pallid clouds; blue spaces undefiled—
Room! give me room! give loneliness and air—
Free things and plenteous in your regions fair.

White dove of David, flying overhead,
   Golden with sunlight on thy snowy wings,
Outspeeding thee my longing thoughts are fled
   To find a home afar from men or things;
Where in His temple, earth o'erarched with sky,
God's heart to mine may speak, my heart reply.

O God of mountains, stars, and boundless spaces,
   O God of freedom and of joyous hearts,
When Thy face looketh forth from all men's faces,
   There will be room enough in crowded marts!
Brood Thou around me, and the noise is o'er,
Thy universe my closet with shut door.

Heart, heart, awake ! The love that loveth all
  Maketh a deeper calm than Horeb's cave,
God in thee, can His children's folly gall !
  Love may be hurt, but shall not love be brave ?—
Thy holy silence sinks in dews of balm ;
Thou art my solitude, my mountain-calm !
George Macdonald.

In spring the green leaves shoot,
In spring the blossoms fall,
With summer falls the fruit,
The leaves in autumn fall,
Contented from the bough
They drop, leaves, blossoms now,
And ripen'd fruit; the warm earth takes them all.

Thus all things ask for rest,
A home above, a home beneath the sod:
The sun will seek the west,
The bird will seek its nest,
The heart another breast
Whereon to lean, the spirit seeks its God.

THE LESSON

I SAID, This task is keen—
But even while I spake, Thou, Love divine
Didst stand behind and gently over-lean
My drooping form, and oh, what task had been
Too stern for feebleness with help of Thine?
Spell Thou this lesson with me line by line,
The sense is rigid, but the voice is dear;
Guide Thou my hand within that hand of Thine,
Thy wounded hand, until its tremblings take
Strength from Thy touch, and even for Thy sake
Trace out each character in outline clear.

ONE FRIEND

Said a sick and lonely child,
"Often have I tired of thee,
Tired of all thy answers mild,
Heard so oft, so wearily;
Wilt thou never tire of me,
Gentle Patience? Now look forth
From our window looking north,
And tell us where the others play,
All this long, warm summer day."

"Love is standing in the sun,
Joy and Beauty at his side,
Now in one their shadows run.
Hope has sent an arrow wide;
Shading from his brow the light,
Now I see him watch its flight."

"Oh, that they would look this way,
Oh, that to this quiet room
They would come awhile to play!
See my rose-tree all in bloom,
See the flowers I dried last spring;
Hear my little linnet sing
In his cage! they need not stay
Longer than they please!" The child
Patience soothed with answer mild.

THE THYME

So spake the hoary thyme,
    Half hidden in the grass :
I watch from morning prime
    Until my Lord shall pass.

How bright beneath the sun,
    How sweet within the glade,
The flow'rets ope, each one
    Beloved by Him who made
His flowers that live in light,
    His flowers that live in shade.

The primroses are pale,
    Yet fair ; the violet grows
Beneath her leafy veil,
    And be she pale none knows,
Or be she fair, so sweet her soul that overflows.

But all my head is strew'd
    With ashes grey ; and bent
Beneath the footfall rude,
    Steals forth my timid scent,
Crush'd from a leaf that curls its wound to hide content.

Why should my Lord delight
    In me ? Behold how fair
His garden is ! How bright
    His roses blooming there ;
His lilies all like queens that know not toil nor care,

In white calm peace on high
    Each rears a blossom'd rod ;
The gentian low doth lie,
    Yet lifts up from the sod
An eye of steadfast blue, that looks up straight to God.

I wait my Lord to greet,
    I can but love and sigh,
I watch His eye to meet,
    He can but pass me by ;
And if His hasty feet
Should crush me, it were sweet
    Beneath His feet to die.

DECLENSION AND REVIVAL

DIE to thy root, sweet flower !
If so God wills, die even to thy root ;
Live there awhile an uncomplaining, mute,
Blank life, with darkness wrapp'd about thy head.
And fear not for the silence round thee spread ;
This is no grave, though thou among the dead
Art counted, but the Hiding-place of Power ;
Die to thy root, sweet flower !

Spring from thy root, sweet flower !
When so God wills, spring even from thy root ;
Send through the earth's warm breast a quicken'd shoot,
Spread to the sunshine, spread unto the shower,

And lift into the sunny air thy dower
Of bloom and odour ; life is on the plains,
And in the woods a sound of birds and rains
That sing together ; lo, the winter's cold
Is past; sweet scents revive, thick buds unfold;
Be thou, too, willing in the day of Power,
Spring from thy root, sweet flower !

THOU hast given me a heart to desire,
Thou hast given me a soul to aspire,
A spirit to question and plead ;
I ask not what Thou hast *decreed ;*
I think but of love and of need ;
Thou art rich, Thou art kind, Thou art free ;
What joy shall be failing to me
Whom Thou lovest ?   Thy smile and Thy kiss
Can give me back all that I miss ;
In Thy presence is fulness of bliss :
I ask not its nature ! I know
It is life, it is youth, it is love,
It is all that is wanting below,
It is all that is waiting above.

Is it peace that I crave ? is it rest ?
Is it love that would bless and be blest ?
Ah, all that Thou takest away,
Thou can'st give me again, in a day,
In an hour, in a moment !   Thy hand
Is full, and I open my breast
For the flower of my soul to expand !

A THOUGHT AT MIDNIGHT

Oh! that some soul o'er-weigh'd
  With love and pity, as a flower with dew,
For me at this still moment wept and pray'd,
And pray'd for me alone! that, leaning through
My casement, now to mine a spirit drew
    So close it scarce could hear
    My secret, nor my tear
    Could feel, nor mark my breast
    That fluttered in unrest,
  Till like two drops that roll
Within each other on the shaken leaf,
Absorb'd and sunk within the tender soul
Of pity, pass'd the shrinking soul of grief!

FAINT YET PURSUING

A SONG OF THE CHURCH MILITANT

All day among the cornfields of the plain,
Reaping a mighty harvest to the Lord,
Our hands have bound the sheaves; we come
    again:
        Shout for the garners stored!

All day among the vineyards of the field
Our feet have trodden out the red ripe vine:
Sing! sing for hearts that have not spared to
    yield
        A yet more purple wine!

All day against the spoilers of our land
Our arms made bare the keen and glittering
    sword;
None turnèd back, none stay'd the lifted hand:
    Sing! sing unto the Lord!

All day beset by spies, begirt with foes,
Building a house of holiness; by night
We watched beside our weapons; slow it rose:
    Sing! sing from Zion's height!

VENI, VENI EMMANUEL

AND art thou come with us to dwell,
Our Prince, our Guide, our Love, our Lord?
And is Thy name Emmanuel,
God present with His world restored?

The world is glad for Thee! the rude
Wild moor, the city's crowded pen;
Each waste, each peopled solitude,
Becomes a home for happy men.

The heart is glad for Thee! it knows
None now shall bid it err or mourn;
And o'er its desert breaks the rose
In triumph o'er the grieving thorn.

Thou bringest all again; with Thee
Is light, is space, is breadth and room
For each thing fair, beloved, and free,
To have its hour of life and bloom.

Each heart's deep instinct unconfess'd,
Each lowly wish, each daring claim;
All, all that life hath long repress'd,
Unfolds, undreading blight or blame.

Thy reign eternal will not cease;
Thy years are sure, and glad, and slow;
Within Thy mighty world of peace
The humblest flower hath leave to blow,

And spread its leaves to meet the sun,
And drink within its soul the dew;
The child's sweet laugh like light may run
Through life's long day, and still be true;

The maid's fond sigh, the lover's kiss,
The firm, warm clasp of constant friend;
And nought shall fail, and nought shall miss
Its blissful aim, its blissful end.

The world is glad for Thee! the heart
Is glad for Thee! and all is well,
And fix'd, and sure, because THOU ART
Whose name is call'd Emmanuel.

Dora Greenwell.

A NEW AND OLD YEAR SONG

PASSING away, saith the World, passing away:
Chances, beauty, and youth sapped day by day:
Thy life never continueth in one stay.
Is the eye waxen dim, is the dark hair changing to grey
That hath won neither laurel nor bay?
I shall clothe myself in spring and bud in May:
Thou, root-stricken, shalt not rebuild thy decay
On my bosom for aye?
Then I answered: Yea.

Passing away, saith my Soul, passing away,
With its burden of fear and hope, of labour and play;
Hearken what the past doth witness and say:
Rust in thy gold, a moth is in thine array,
A canker is in thy bud, thy leaf must decay.
At midnight, at cockcrow, at morning, one certain day,
Lo, the Bridegroom shall come and shall not delay:
Watch thou and pray.
Then I answered: Yea.

Passing away, saith my God, passing away:
Winter passeth after the long delay:
New grapes on the vine, new figs on the tender spray,
Turtle calleth turtle in Heaven's May.
Though I tarry, wait for Me, trust Me, watch and pray.
Arise, come away, night is past, and lo, it is day,
My love, My sister, My spouse, thou shalt hear Me say.
Then I answered: Yea.

A BRUISED REED

I WILL accept thy will to do and be,
   Thy hatred and intolerance of sin,
Thy will at least to love, that burns within
     And thirsteth after Me:
So will I render fruitful, blessing still,
   The germs and small beginnings in thy heart,
   Because thy will cleaves to the better part.—
     Alas, I cannot will.

Dost not thou will, poor soul? Yet I receive
   The inner unseen longings of the soul,
I guide them turning towards Me; I control
     And charm hearts till they grieve:

If thou desire, it yet shall come to pass,
  Though thou but wish indeed to choose My
    love;
  For I have power in earth and heaven above.—
    I cannot wish, alas!

What, neither choose nor wish to choose! and yet
  I still must strive to win thee and constrain:
For thee I hung upon the cross in pain,
    How then can I forget?
If thou as yet dost neither love, nor hate,
  Nor choose, nor wish,—resign thyself, be still
  Till I infuse love, hatred, longing, will.—
    I do not deprecate.

FROM HOUSE TO HOME

Then earth and heaven were rolled up like a
    scroll;
  Time and space, change and death, had
    passed away;
Weight, number, measure, each had reached
    its whole;
  The day had come, that day.

Multitudes—multitudes—stood up in bliss,
  Made equal to the angels, glorious, fair;
With harps, palms, wedding-garments, kiss of
    peace,
  And crowned and haloed hair.

They sang a song, a new song in the height,
    Harping with harps to Him who is strong
        and true:
They drank new wine, their eyes saw with new
    light,
    Lo, all things were made new.

Tier beyond tier they rose and rose, and rose
    So high that it was dreadful, flames with
        flames:
No man could number them, no tongue disclose
    Their secret sacred names.

As though one pulse stirred all, one rush of blood
    Fed all, one breath swept through them
        myriad-voiced,
They struck their harps, cast down their
    crowns, they stood
    And worshipped and rejoiced.

Each face looked one way like a moon new-lit,
    Each face looked one way towards its Sun of
        Love;
Drank love, and bathed in love, and mirrored it,
    And knew no end thereof.

Glory touched glory on each blessèd head,
    Hand locked dear hands never to sunder more,
These were the new-begotten from the dead
    Whom the great birthday bore.

Heart answered heart, soul answered soul at rest
   Double against each other, filled, sufficed:
All loving, loved of all; but loving best
   And best beloved of Christ.

"THE WILL OF THE LORD BE DONE"

O Lord, fulfil Thy will,
Be the days few or many, good or ill:
Prolong them, to suffice
For offering up ourselves Thy sacrifice;
Shorten them if Thou wilt,
To make in righteousness an end of guilt.
Yea, they will not be long
To souls who learn to sing a patient song;
Yea, short they will not be
To souls on tiptoe to flee home to Thee.
O Lord, fulfil Thy will:
Make Thy will ours, and keep us patient still,
Be the days few or many, good or ill.

"THAT WHERE I AM, THERE YE MAY BE ALSO"

How know I that it looms lovely, that land I
   have never seen,
With morning-glories, and heartsease, and un-
   exampled green,

With neither heat nor cold in the balm-redolent
    air ?
  Some of this, not all, I know ; but this is so :
        Christ is there.

How know I that blessedness befalls who dwell
    in paradise,
The outwearied hearts refreshing, rekindling
    the worn-out eyes,
All souls singing, seeing, rejoicing everywhere ?
  Nay, much more than this I know ; for this
    is so :
        Christ is there.

O Lord Christ, whom having not seen I love
    and desire to love,
O Lord Christ, who lookest on me uncomely,
    yet still Thy dove,
Take me to Thee in paradise, Thine own made
    fair ;
  For whatever else I know, this thing is so :
        Thou art there.

    Sooner or later : yet at last
    The Jordan must be past ;

    It may be he will overflow
    His banks the day we go ;

    It may be that his cloven deep
    Will stand up as an heap.

Sooner or later : yet one day
We all must pass that way ;

Each man, each woman, humbled, pale,
Pass veiled within the veil ;

Child, parent, bride, companion,
Alone, alone, alone.

For none a ransom can be paid,
A suretyship be made :

I, bent by mine own burden, must
Enter my house of dust ;

I, rated to the full amount,
Must render mine account.

When earth and sea shall empty all
Their graves of great and small ;

When earth wrapped in a fiery flood
Shall no more hide her blood ;

When mysteries shall be revealed ;
All secrets be unsealed ;

When things of night, when things of shame
Shall find at last a name,

Pealed for a hissing and a curse
Throughout the universe :

Then awful Judge, most awful God,
Then cause to bud Thy rod,

To bloom with blossoms, and to give
Almonds ; yea, bid us live.

I plead Thyself with Thee, I plead
Thee in our utter need :

Jesus, most merciful of men,
Show mercy on us then ;

Lord God of mercy and of men
Show mercy on us then.

A CHILL blank world. Yet over the utmost sea
The light of a coming dawn is rising to me,
   No more than a paler shade of darkness as yet ;
While I lift my heart, O Lord, my heart unto Thee
   Who hast not forgotten me, yea, who wilt not forget.

Forget not Thy sorrowful servant, O Lord my God,
Weak as I cry, faint as I cry underneath Thy rod,
   Soon to lie dumb before Thee, a body devoid of breath,
Dust to dust, ashes to ashes, a sod to the sod :
   Forget not my life, O my Lord, forget not my death.

O FOOLISH soul! to make thy count
   For languid falls and much forgiven,
When like a flame thou mightest mount
   To storm and carry heaven.

A life so faint,—is this to live?
   A goal so mean,—is this a goal?
Christ love thee, remedy, forgive,
   Save thee, O foolish soul.

"A VAIN SHADOW"

THE world,—what a world, ah me!
   Mouldy, worm-eaten, grey;
Vain as a leaf from a tree,
   As a fading day,
As veriest vanity,
   As the froth and the spray
Of the hollow-billowed sea,
As what was and shall not be,
   As what is and passes away.
Christina Rossetti.

S. PAUL *speaks*

God, who at sundry times in manners many
    Spake to the fathers and is speaking still,
Eager to find if ever or if any
    Souls will obey and hearken to His will,—

Who that one moment has the least descried Him,
    Dimly and faintly, hidden and afar,
Doth not despise all excellence beside Him,
    Pleasures and powers that are not and that are,—

Ay amid all men bear himself thereafter,
    Smit with a solemn and a sweet surprise,
Dumb to their scorn, and turning on their laughter
    Only the dominance of earnest eyes ?—

God, who, whatever frenzy of our fretting
    Vexes sad life to spoil and to destroy,
Lendeth an hour for peace and for forgetting,
    Setteth in pain the jewel of his joy :—

Gentle and faithful, tyrannous and tender,
  Ye that have known Him, is He sweet to know?
Softy He touches, for the reed is slender,
  Wisely enkindles, for the flame is low.

God, who when Enoch from the earth was hidden
  Saved him from death, and Noë from the sea,
Chose Him a people for His purpose bidden,
  Found in Chaldæa the elect Chaldee,—

God, who, His promise thro' the ages keeping,
  Called him from Charran, summoned him from Ur,
Gave to his wife a laughter and a weeping,
  Light to the nations and a son for her,—

God, who in Israel's bondage and bewailing
  Heard them and granted them their heart's desire,
Clave them the deep with power and with prevailing,
  Gloomed in the cloud and glowed into the fire,

Fed them with manna, furnished with a fountain,
  Followed with waves the raising of the rod,
Drew them and drave, till Moses on the mountain
  Died of the kisses of the lips of God ;—

God, who was not in earth when it was shaken,
    Could not be found in fury of the flame,
Then to His seer, the faithful and forsaken,
    Softly was manifest and spake by name,

Showed him a remnant barred from the betrayal,
    Close in his Carmel, where the caves are dim,
So many knees that had not bent to Baal,
    So many mouths that had not kissèd him,—

God, who to glean the vineyard of His choosing
    Sent them evangelists till day was done,
Bore with the churls, their wrath and their refusing,—
    Gave at the last the glory of His Son :—

Lo, as in Eden, when the days were seven,
    Pison thro' Havilah that softly ran
Bare on his breast the changes of the heaven,
    Felt on his shores the silence of a man :

Silence, for Adam, when the day departed
    Left him in twilight with his charge to keep,
Careless and confident and single-hearted,
    Trusted in God and turned himself to sleep :

Then in the midnight stirring in his slumber
    Opened his vision on the heights and saw
New without name or ordinance or number,
    Set for á marvel, silent for an awe,

Stars in the firmament above him beaming,
    Stars in the firmament, alive and free,
Stars, and of stars the innumerable streaming,
    Deep in the deeps, a river in the sea ;—

These as he watched thro' march of their arising,
    Many in multitudes and one by one,
Somewhat from God with a superb surprising
    Breathed in his eyes the promise of the sun.

So tho' our Daystar from our sight be taken,
    Gone from His brethren, hidden from His own,
Yet in His setting are we not forsaken,
    Suffer not shadows of the dark alone.

Not in the west is Thine appearance ended,
    Neither from dark shall Thy renewal be,
Lo, for the firmament in spaces splendid
    Lighteth her beacon-fires ablaze for Thee :

Holds them and hides and drowns them and discovers,
    Throngs them together, kindles them afar,
Showeth, O Love, Thy multitude of lovers,
    Souls that shall know Thee and the saints that are.

Look what a company of constellations !
    Say, can the sky so many lights contain?
Hath the great earth these endless generations?
    Are there so many purified thro' pain ?

Witness the wonder when Thy saints assembled
   Waited the message, and the message came;
Ay with hearts tremulous and house that trembled,
   Ay with the Paraclete that fell in flame.

Witness the men whom with a word he gaineth,
   Bold who were base and voiceful who were dumb :—
Battle, I know, so long as life remaineth,
   Battle for all, but these have overcome.

Witness the women, of His children sweetest,—
   Scarcely earth seeth them, but earth shall see,—
Thou in their woe Thine agony completest,
   Christ, and their solitude is nigh to Thee.

What is this psalm from pitiable places
   Glad where the messengers of peace have trod ;
Whose are these beautiful and holy faces
   Lit with their loving and aflame with God?

Eager and faint, impassionate and lonely,
   These in their hour shall prophesy again :
This is His will who hath endured, and only
   Sendeth the promise where He sends the pain.

Ay unto these distributeth the Giver
    Sorrow and sanctity, and loves them well,
Grants them a power and passion to deliver
    Hearts from the prison-house and souls from hell.

Thinking hereof, I wot not if the portal
    Opeth already to my Lord above:
Lo, there is no more mortal and immortal,
    Nought is on earth or in the heavens but love.

Surely He cometh, and a thousand voices
    Call to the saints and to the deaf are dumb;
Surely He cometh, and the earth rejoices,
    Glad in His coming who hath sworn, I come.

This hath He done, and shall we not adore Him?
    This shall He do, and can we still despair?
Come, let us quickly fling ourselves before Him,
    Cast at His feet the burthen of our care,

Flash from our eyes the glow of our thanksgiving,
    Glad and regretful, confident and calm,
Then thro' all life, and what is after living,
    Thrill to the tireless music of a psalm.

Yea, thro' life, death, thro' sorrow and thro' sinning,
He shall suffice me, for He hath sufficed :
Christ is the end, for Christ was the beginning,
Christ the beginning, for the end is Christ.

Frederick Myers.

Ah, that sharp thrill through all my frame!
    And yet once more! Withstand
I can no longer; in Thy name
    I yield me to Thy hand.

Such pangs were in the soul unborn,
    The fear, the joy were such,
When first it felt in that keen morn
    A dread creating touch.

Maker of man, Thy pressure sure
    This grosser stuff must quell;
The spirit faints, yet will endure;
    Subdue, control, compel.

The Potter's finger shaping me—
    Praise, praise! the clay curves up
Not for dishonour, though it be
    God's least adornèd cup.

A SPEAKER TO GOD

Thus it shall be a lifetime,—ne'er to meet;
  A trackless land divides us lone and long;
Others who seek Him find, run swift to greet
  Their Friend, approach the Bridegroom's door with song.

I stand, nor dare affirm I see or hear;
  How should I dream, when strict is my employ?
Yet if some time, far hence, Thou drawest near,
  Shall there be any joy like to our joy?
Edward Dowden.

BARNFLOOR AND WINEPRESS

"If the Lord do not help thee, whence shall I help thee out of the barnfloor, or out of the wine-press?"—
2 KINGS vi. 27.

Thou who on Sin's wages starvest,
Behold we have the Joy of Harvest:
For us was gathered the First-fruits,
For us was lifted from the roots,
Sheaved in cruel bands, bruised sore,
Scourged upon the threshing-floor,
Where the upper millstone roofed His Head,
At morn we found the Heavenly Bread;
And on a thousand altars laid,
Christ our Sacrifice is made.

Thou, whose dry plot for moisture gapes,
We shout with them that tread the grapes;
For us the Vine was fenced with thorn,
Five ways the precious branches torn.
Terrible fruit was on the tree
In the acre of Gethsemane:
For us by Calvary's distress
The Wine was rackèd from the press;
Now, in our altar-vessels stored,
Lo, the sweet Vintage of the Lord!

In Joseph's garden they threw by
The riven Vine, leafless, lifeless, dry:
On Easter morn the Tree was forth,
In forty days reached Heaven from earth,—
Soon the whole world is overspread:
Ye weary, come into the shade.

The field where He hath planted us
Shall shake her fruit as Libanus,
When He has sheaved us in His sheaf,
When He has made us bear His leaf.
We scarcely call that banquet food,
But even our Saviour's and our blood,
We are so grafted on His wood.

GOD'S GRANDEUR

The world is charged with the grandeur of God.
   It will flame out, like shining from shook foil,
   It gathers to a greatness like the ooze of oil
Crushed. Why do men then now not reck His rod?
Generations have trod, have trod, have trod;
   And all is seared with trade; bleared, smeared with toil;
   And bears man's smudge, and shares man's smell; the soil
Is bare now, nor can foot feel being shod.

And for all this, nature is never spent ;
  There lives the dearest freshness deep down
    things ;
And though the last lights from the black west
    went,
  Oh, morning at the brown brink eastwards
    springs—
Because the Holy Ghost over the bent
  World broods with warm breast, and with,
    ah, bright wings.

HEAVEN HAVEN

(A NUN TAKES THE VEIL)

I HAVE desired to go
  Where springs not fail,
To fields where flies no sharp and sided hail,
  And a few lilies blow.

And I have asked to be
  Where no storms come,
Where the green swell is in the havens dumb,
  And out of the swing of the sea.

MORNING, MIDDAY, AND EVENING SACRIFICE

The dappled die-away
Cheek and wimpled lip,
The gold-wisp, the airy-grey
Eye, all in fellowship—
This, all this, beauty blooming,
This, all this, freshness fuming,
Give God while worth consuming.

Both thought and thew now bolder
And told by Nature tower;
Head, heart, hand, heel, and shoulder
That beat and breathe in power—
This pride of prime's enjoyment
Take as for tool, not toy meant,
And hold at Christ's employment.

The vault and scope and schooling,
And mastery in the mind,
In silk ash, kept from cooling,
And ripest under rind—
What Death half lifts the latch of,
What Hell stalks towards the snatch of,
Your offering, with despatch, of!

Gerard Hopkins.

JOY

Joy, sweetest lifeborn Joy, where dost thou dwell?
Upon the formless moments of our being
Flitting, to mock the ear that heareth well,
To escape the trainèd eye that strains in seeing,
Dost thou fly with us whither we are fleeing;
Or home in our creations, to withstand
Black-wingèd Death, that slays the making hand?

The making mind, that must untimely perish
Amidst its work which time may not destroy,
The beauteous forms which man shall love to
    cherish,
The glorious songs that combat Earth's annoy?
Thou dost dwell here, I know, divinest Joy:
But they who build thy towers fair and strong,
Of all that toil, feel most of care and wrong.

Sense is so tender, oh, and hope so high,
That common pleasures mock their hope and
    sense;
And swifter than doth lightning from the sky
The ecstasy they pine for flashes hence,
Leaving the darkness and the woe immense,
Wherewith it seems no thread of life was woven,
Nor doth the track remain where once 'twas
    cloven.

And heaven and all the stable elements
That guard God's purpose mock us, though the
    mind
Be spent in searching : for His old intents
We see were never for our joy designed :
They shine as doth the bright sun on the blind,
Or like His pensioned stars, that hymn above
His praise, but not toward us, that God is love.

For who so well hath wooed the maiden hours
As quite to have won the worth of their rich
    show,
To rob the night of mystery, or the flowers
Of their sweet delicacy ere they go ?
Nay, even the dear occasion when we know,
We miss the joy, and on the gliding day
The special glories float and pass away.

Only Life's common plod : still to repair
The body and the thing which perisheth :
The soil, the smutch, the toil and ache and wear,
The grinding enginry of blood and breath,
Pain's random darts, the heartless spade of
    Death :
All is but grief, and heavily we call
On the last terror for the end of all.

Then comes the happy moment : not a stir
In any tree, no portent in the sky :
The morn doth neither hasten nor defer,
The morrow hath no name to call it by,

But life and joy are one,—we know not why,—
As though our very blood long breathless lain
Had tasted of the breath of God again.

And having tasted it I speak of it,
And praise Him thinking how I trembled then
When His touch strengthened me, as now I sit
In wonder, reaching out beyond my ken,
Reaching to turn the day back, and my pen
Urging to tell a tale which told would seem
The witless phantasy of them that dream.

But O most blessèd truth, for truth thou art,
Abide thou with me till my life shall end.
Divinity hath surely touched my heart;
I have possessed more joy than earth can lend:
I may attain what time shall never spend.
Only let not my duller days destroy
The memory of thy witness and my joy.

Since to be loved endures,
    To love is wise:
Earth hath no good but yours,
    Brave, joyful eyes:

Earth hath no sin but thine,
    Dull eye of scorn:
O'er thee the sun doth pine
    And angels mourn.

This world is unto God a work of art,
Of which the unaccomplished heavenly plan
Lives in His masterpiece, and grows with man
Unto perfection and success in part.
The ultimate creation stayed to start
From the last creature for whom all began:
Who, child in what he is and what he can,
Hath yet God's judgment and desire at heart.

Knowledge denied him, and his little skill
Cumbered by laws he never can annul,
Baffled by qualities adverse and ill,
With feeble hands, few years, and senses dull,
His art is Nature's nature, and love still
Makes his abode with the most beautiful.

When I see childhood on the threshold seize
The prize of life from age and likelihood,
I mourn time's change that will not be withstood,
Thinking how Christ said, *Be like one of these.*
For in the forest among many trees
Scarce one in all is found that hath made good
The virgin pattern of its slender wood,
That courtesied in joy to every breeze;

But scathed, but knotted trunks that raise on high
Their arms in stiff contortion, strained and bare:
Whose crowns in patriarchal sorrow sigh.
So little children ye—nay, nay, ye ne'er
From me shall learn how sure the change and nigh,
When ye shall share our strength and mourn to share.

THESE meagre rhymes which a returning mood
Sometimes o'errateth, I as oft despise:
And knowing them ill-natured, stiff, and rude,
See them as others with contemptuous eyes.
Nay, and I wonder less at God's respect
For man, a minim jot in time and space,
Than at the soaring faith of His elect,
That gift of gifts, the comfort of His grace.

O work unsearchable, O heavenly love,
Most infinitely tender, so to touch
The work that we can meanly reckon of:
Surely—I say—we are favoured overmuch.
But of this wonder, what doth most amaze
Is that we know our love is held for praise.

PATER NOSTER

Eternal Father, who didst all create,
In whom we live and to whose bosom move,
To all men be Thy name known which is Love,
Till its loud praises sound at heaven's high gate.
Perfect Thy kingdom in our passing state,
That here on earth Thou mayest as well approve
Our service as Thou ownest theirs above,
Whose joy we echo and in pain await.

Grant body and soul each day their daily bread :
And should in spite of grace fresh woe begin,
Even as our anger soon is past and dead
Be Thy remembrance mortal of our sin :
By Thee in paths of peace Thy sheep be led,
And in the vale of terror comforted.

LAUS DEO

Let praise devote thy work, and skill employ
Thy whole mind, and thy heart be lost in joy.
Well-doing bringeth pride, this constant thought
Humility, that thy best done is nought.
Man doeth nothing well, be it great or small,
Save to praise God ; but that hath savèd all :
For God requires no more than thou hast done,
And takes thy work to bless it for His own.
Robert Bridges.

THE SHRINE

THERE is a shrine whose golden gate
Was opened by the Hand of God ;
It stands serene, inviolate,
Though millions have its pavement trod ;
As fresh as when the first sunrise
Awoke the lark in Paradise.

'Tis compass'd with the dust and toil
Of common days, yet should there fall
A single speck, a single soil,
Upon the whiteness of its wall,
The angels' tears in tender rain
Would make the temple theirs again.

Without, the world is tired and old,
But once within the enchanted door,
The mists of time are backward rolled,
And creeds and ages are no more,
But all the human-hearted meet
In one communion vast and sweet.

I enter ; all is simply fair,
Nor incense clouds, nor carven throne,
But in the fragrant morning air
A gentle lady sits alone ;
My mother—ah ! whom should I see
Within, save ever only thee ?

"OSCULO ORIS SUI OSCULETUR ME"

CHRIST, for whose only love I keep me clean
Among the palaces of Babylon,
I would not Thou should'st reckon me with them,
Who miserly would count each golden stone
That flags the street of Thy Jerusalem;—
Who having touched and tasted, heard and seen,

Half drunken yet from earthly revelries,
Would wipe with flower-wreath'd hair Thy bleeding feet,
Jostling about Thee, but to stay the heat
Of pale parch'd lips in Thy cool chalices.

"Our cups are emptiness, how long, how long,
Before that Thou wilt pour us of Thy wine?
Thy sweet new wine, that we may thirst no more.
Our lamps are darkness, open day of Thine;
Surely is light to spare behind that door
Where God is sun, and saints a starry throng."

But I, how little profit were to me
Though mine the twelve foundations of the skies,
With this green world of love an age below?—
The soft remembrance of those Human Eyes

Would pale the everlasting jewel-glow,
And o'er the perfect, passionless minstrelsy

A voice would sound, the decachords above,
Deadening the music of the living land :—
Thou mad'st, Thou knowest, Thou wilt understand,
And stay me with the apples of Thy love.

My Christ, remember that betrothal day ;—
" Blessed be He that cometh " was the song ;
Glad as the Hebrew boys who cried Hosanna,
O'er hearts thick strewn with palms they pass'd along,
To reap in might the fields of heavenly manna ;
These were the bridesmen in their white array.

Soon hearts and eyes were lifted up to Thee,
Deep in dim glories of the sanctuary,
Between the thunderous alleluia-praise ;
Through incense-hazes that encompassed Thee,
I saw the priestly hands Thyself upraise—
Heaven sank to earth, earth leapt to heaven for me.

Rise, Peter, rise, He standeth on the shore,
The thrice-denied of Pilate's judgment hall,
His hand is o'er the shingle, lest thou fall,
He wipes thy bitter tears for evermore.

Lovest Thou? My Belovèd, answer me;
Of Thine all-knowledge show me only this—
Tarrieth the answer?   Lo, the House of Bread,
Lo, God and Man made one in Mary's kiss,
Bending in rapture o'er the manger bed :
I with the holy kings will go and see.

REQUESTS

I ASKED for Peace,—
My sins arose
And bound me close,
I could not find release.

I asked for Truth,—
My doubts came in,
And with their din
They wearied all my youth.

I asked for Love,—
My lovers failed,
And griefs assailed
Around, beneath, above.

I asked for Thee,—
And Thou didst come
To take me home,
Within Thy heart to be.
Digby Mackworth-Dolben.

THE CELESTIAL SURGEON

If I have faltered more or less
In my great task of happiness ;
If I have moved among my race
And shown no glorious morning face ;
If beams from happy human eyes
Have moved me not ; if morning skies,
Books, and my food, and summer rain
Knocked on my sullen heart in vain :
Lord, thy most pointed pleasure take
And stab my spirit broad awake ;
Or, Lord, if too obdurate I,
Choose Thou, before that spirit die,
A piercing pain, a killing sin,
And to my dead heart run them in !

THE HOUSE BEAUTIFUL

A naked house, a naked moor,
A shivering pool before the door.
A garden bare of flowers and fruit,
And poplars at the garden foot;
Such is the place that I live in,
Bleak without and bare within.

Yet shall your ragged moor receive
The incomparable pomp of eve,
And the cold glories of the dawn
Behind your shivering trees be drawn;
And when the wind from place to place
Doth the unmoored cloud-galleons chase,
Your garden gloom and gleam again,
With leaping sun, with glancing rain.
Here shall the wizard moon ascend
The heavens, in the crimson end
Of day's declining splendour; here
The army of the stars appear.
The neighbour hollows, dry or wet,
Spring shall with tender flowers beset;
And oft the morning muser see
Larks rising from the broomy lea,
And every fairy wheel and thread
Of cobweb dew-bediamonded.
When daisies go, shall winter-time
Silver the simple grass with rime;

Autumnal frosts enchant the pool,
And make the cart-ruts beautiful;
And when snow-bright the moor expands,
How shall your children clap their hands!
To make this earth, our hermitage,
A cheerful and a changeful page,
God's bright and intricate device
Of days and seasons doth suffice.
Robert Louis Stevenson.

THE HOUND OF HEAVEN

I FLED Him, down the nights and down the
    days ;
  I fled Him, down the arches of the years ;
I fled Him, down the labyrinthine ways
    Of my own mind ; and in the mist of tears
I hid from Him, and under running laughter.
        Up vistaed hopes I sped ;
        And shot, precipitated
Adown Titanic glooms of chasmed fears,
    From those strong feet that followed, followed
        after.
        But with unhurrying chase,
        And unperturbèd pace,
Deliberate speed, majestic instancy,
        They beat—and a voice beat
        More instant than the feet ;
"All things betray thee, who betrayest Me."

        I pleaded outlaw-wise,
By many a hearted casement, curtained red,
    Trellised with intertwining charities ;
(For, though I knew His love who followèd,
        Yet was I sore adread
Lest, having Him, I must have naught beside)
But, if one little casement parted wide,

The gust of His approach would clash it to.
Fear wist not to evade, as Love wist to pursue.
Across the margent of the world I fled,
  And troubled the gold gateways of the stars,
  Smiting for shelter on their changèd bars ;
    Fretted to dulcet jars
And silvern chatter the pale ports o' the moon.
I said to dawn : Be sudden—to eve : Be soon ;
With thy young skiey blossoms heap me over
    From this tremendous Lover !
Float thy vague veil about me, lest He see !
  I tempted all His servitors, but to find
My own betrayal in their constancy,
In faith to Him their fickleness to me,
  Their traitorous trueness, and their loyal deceit.
To all swift things for swiftness did I sue ;
  Clung to the whistling mane of every wind.
    But whether they swept, smoothly fleet,
    The long savannahs of the blue ;
      Or whether, thunder-driven,
    They clanged his chariot 'thwart a heaven,
Plashy with flying lightnings round the spurn o' their feet :
  Fear wist not to evade as Love wist to pursue.
    Still with unhurrying chase,
    And unperturbèd pace,
Deliberate speed, majestic instancy,
Came on the following Feet,
And a Voice above their beat—
"Nought shelters thee, who wilt not shelter Me."

I sought no more that, after which I strayed,
   In face of man or maid;
But still within the little children's eyes
   Seems something, something that replies,
They at least are for me, surely for me!
I turned me to them very wistfully;
But just as their young eyes grew sudden fair
   With dawning answers there,
Their angel plucked them from me by the hair.
" Come then, ye other children, Nature's—share
With me " (said I) " your delicate fellowship;
   Let me greet you lip to lip,
   Let me twine with you caresses,
      Wantoning
   With our Lady-Mother's vagrant tresses,
      Banqueting
   With her in her wind-walled palace,
   Underneath her azured daïs,
   Quaffing, as your taintless way is,
      From a chalice
Lucent-weeping out of the dayspring."
      So it was done:
I in their delicate fellowship was one—
Drew the bolt of Nature's secrecies.
   I knew all the swift importings
   On the wilful face of skies;
   I knew how the clouds arise
   Spumèd of the wild sea-snortings;
      All that's born or dies
   Rose and drooped with—made them shapers

Of mine own moods, or wailful or divine,
   With them joyed and was bereaven.
   I was heavy with the even,
   When she lit her glimmering tapers
   Round the day's dead sanctities:
   I laughed in the morning's eyes,
I triumphed and I saddened with all weather;
         Heaven and I wept together,
And its sweet tears were salt with mortal mine;
Against the red throb of its sunset heart
         I laid my own to beat,
         And share commingling heat;
But not by that, by that, was eased my human smart.
In vain my tears were wet on Heaven's grey cheek,
For ah! we know not what each other says,
   These things and I; in sound *I* speak,
Their sound is but their stir, they speak by silences.
Nature, poor stepdame, cannot slake my drought;
   Let her, if she would owe me,
Drop yon blue bosom-veil of sky, and show me
   The breasts o' her tenderness:
Never did any milk of hers once bless
         My thirsting mouth.
         Nigh and nigh draws the chase,
         With unperturbèd pace,

Deliberate speed, majestic instancy;
  And past those noisèd Feet,
  A Voice comes yet more fleet;
"Lo! naught contents thee, who content'st not Me."

Naked I wait Thy love's uplifted stroke!
My harness piece by piece Thou hast hewn from me,
  And smitten me to my knee;
I am defenceless utterly.
I slept, methinks, and woke,
And, slowly gazing, find me stripped in sleep.
In the rash lustihead of my young powers,
  I shook the pillaring hours
And pulled my life upon me; grimed with smears,
I stand amid the dust o' the mounded years;
My mangled youth lies dead beneath the heap,
My days have crackled and gone up in smoke,
Have puffed and burst as sun-starts on a stream.
  Yea, faileth now even dream
The dreamer, and the lute the lutanist;
Even the linked fantasies, in whose blossomy twist
I swung the earth a trinket at my wrist,
Are yielding: cords of all too weak account
For earth with heavy griefs so overplussed.
  Ah! is Thy love indeed
A weed, albeit an amaranthine weed,
Suffering no flowers except its own to mount?

  Ah! must—
  Designer infinite!
Ah! must thou char the wood ere thou canst
  limn with it?
My freshness spent its wavering shower i' the
  dust;
And now my heart is as a broken fount,
Wherein tear-drippings stagnate, spilt down
  ever
 From the dank thoughts that shiver
Upon the sighful branches of my mind.
  Such is; what is to be?
The pulp so bitter, how shall taste the rind?
I dimly guess what Time in mists confounds;
Yet ever and anon a trumpet sounds
From the hid battlements of Eternity,
Those shaken mists a space unsettle, then
Round the half-glimpsèd turrets slowly wash
  again;
 But not ere him who summoneth
 I first have seen, enwound
With glooming robes purpureal, cypress-
  crowned;
His name I know, and what his trumpet
  saith.
Whether man's heart or life it be which
  yields
 Thee harvest, must Thy harvest fields
  Be dunged with rotten death?
   Now of that long pursuit
   Comes on at hand the bruit;

That Voice is round me like a bursting sea—
      "And is thy earth so marred,
        Shattered in shard on shard?
Lo, all things fly thee, for thou fliest Me!

   "Strange, piteous, futile thing!
Wherefore should any set thee love apart?
Seeing none but I makes much of naught" (He said),
"And human love needs human meriting:
      How hast thou merited—
Of all man's clotted clay the dingiest clot?
      Alack, thou knowest not
How little worthy of any love thou art!
Whom wilt thou find to love ignoble thee,
      Save Me, save only Me?
All which I took from thee I did but take,
      Not for thy harms,
But just that thou might'st seek it in My arms.
      All which thy child's mistake
Fancies as lost, I have stored for thee at home:
      Rise, clasp My hand, and come."

      Halts by me that footfall:
      Is my gloom, after all,
Shade of His hand, outstretched caressingly?
      "Ah, fondest, blindest, weakest,
      I am He whom thou seekest!
Thou dravest love from thee, who dravest Me!"

Francis Thompson.

NOTES

THE three anonymous poems which open our anthology are taken from an early fifteenth-century MS. in Lambeth Library. They were first printed by the Early English Text Society in 1866-67, and are now offered, slightly modernised, to the general reader. Dr. Furnivall has very kindly revised the proof, and added a few scansion marks.

P. 11.—From *Troylus and Criseyde*, v. ad. fin. *Repaireth, upcasteth*, etc., are imperatives.

P. 12.—The conclusion of Ralegh's "Pilgrimage," which may be found in Hannah's *Courtly Poets*, is here omitted, both because "nectar suckets" and "crystal buckets" are intolerably quaint to us, and also because Ralegh's indictment of the administration of justice in his day is happily without application to ours.

P. 14.—"The Ministry of Angels" is from the "Faerie Queene," II. viii. 1, 2; "The Love of Christ" from "A Hymn of Heavenly Love."

P. 19.—This Sonnet concludes the series of "Sonnets to Stella."

P. 20.—From *Cælica*, Sonnet xcvii. Lord Brooke was the intimate friend and companion of Sir Philip Sidney, and shared his literary tastes. His own writing is usually very crabbed, but it is full of thought, and often startlingly modern. Here is a verse on "Inconsistency" from "A Treatise of Warres," of which Coleridge was fond:

> "God and the world they worship still together:
> Draw not their laws to Him, but His to theirs;
> Untrue to both, so prosperous in neither;
> Amid their own desires still raising fears;
> Unwise, as all distracted powers be;
> Strangers to God, fools to humanity.
> Too good for great things and too great for good," etc.

P. 21.—Southwell was a Jesuit priest who was executed under Elizabeth's Acts against the Romanists after being "thirteen times most cruelly tortured" to make him confess with whom he had been hiding. His best-known poems are "The Burning Babe," and others upon the Nativity, where his quaintness is less out of place than in penitential verse. His longest effort, "St. Peter's Complaint," though by no means without genuine feeling, is hard to read, owing to the merciless coruscation of conceits, and the monotony arising from over-elaborate balance and want of variety in the pause. There are also occasional lapses in taste. But, compared with Crashaw, his sentimental peccadilloes are inconsiderable. Now and then he writes a perfect epigram, as in the final couplet of "Scorn not the Least"—

"We trample grass, and prize the flowers of May,
Yet grass is green when flowers do fade away."

P. 24.—"Faith and Form" is from "Musophilus"; "Works" from "Epistle to Sir Thomas Egerton." Daniel's readers would probably be increased by hundreds, if there were a modern edition of his poems. His writing, to quote Dr. Macdonald, is "full of the practical wisdom of the inner life." Two lines of the "Epistle to the Countess of Cumberland" have become part of our circulating medium in moral ideas—

"Unless above himself he can
Erect himself, how poor a thing is man."

Coleridge says of him, "Read Daniel, the admirable Daniel; the style and language are just such as any very pure and manly writer of the present day—Wordsworth, for example—would use; it seems quite modern in comparison with the style of Shakespeare."—(*Table Talk*, Bohn's ed., p. 278).

P. 26.—Sir John Davies (1569-1626) is one of the more successful of our philosophical poets. The first passage here chosen is from the close of his poem "Of the Soul of Man and the Immortality thereof," which is the second part of "Nosce Teipsum." The two verses on "Self Knowledge" are from the first part.

P. 28.—Sir Henry Wotton (1568-1639), whose life is so charmingly told by Izaak Walton, is probably best known now by his poem on the Queen of Bohemia. But his religious verse is of no mean order. His life was passed in diplomacy, chiefly at Venice; he was the author of the famous epigram, "An ambassador is an honest man, sent to lie abroad for the good of his country"; *to lie* being the technical term for an ambassador's residence. In old age he became Provost of Eton. Milton's "Comus" is preceded by a delightful letter from him, written the year before his death.

P. 29.—*The world's contracted sum.* References to the theory that man was a "microcosm" are not unfrequent in Shakespeare: *Coriolanus*, ii. 1, 55; *Lear*, iii. 1, 10; *Richard II.*, v. 5, 9. Cf. Sir Thomas Browne, *Religio Medici*, ii. 11: "The world that I regard is myself; it is the microcosm of my own frame that I rest mine eye on."

P. 32.—Donne's memory is preserved to this generation, more by Walton's Life than by his own writings, though these will never lack a few devoted admirers. Among the fragments preserved by Drummond of Ben Jonson's talk are one or two judgments about Donne which are worth quoting:—"He esteemeth John Donne the first poet in the world in some things ... that Donne for not keeping of accent deserved hanging ... that Donne himself, for not being understood, would perish." There is a characteristic flavour about everything Donne wrote, but there are very few pieces on which one would care to stake his reputation; commonly either the thought bolts round the corner after some conceit, or the verse grows halting. Perhaps his most perfect religious piece is the "Hymn to God the Father" here quoted. The reader, however, who studies Donne attentively will not lose or regret his labour; the thought is worth digging for, and the expression, if recondite, often singularly telling and beautiful.

P. 35, line 5.—A reference to the traditional explanation of the name Adam—"red earth"; the poet would say that the "Old Adam" still dwells in his heart.

P. 36.—I cannot convince myself that the fifth line of the last stanza does not contain a pun on his own name, which was pronounced like "done." Walton tells us "that he caused it to be set to a most grave and solemn tune, and to be often sung to the organ by the choristers of St. Paul's Church in his own hearing, especially at the evening service, and at his return from his customary devotions in that place did occasionally say to a friend, 'The words of this hymn have restored to me the same thoughts of joy that possessed my soul in my sickness when I composed it.'"

P. 37.—"Hymn to God." This is a portion of the hymn composed on his deathbed.

"Good Friday." By "my soul's form" Donne means "the natural motion of the soul"; this is overruled by the business that takes him westward.

P. 39.—"Easter Day," line 13. This couplet means that Christ after His resurrection was enabled to make others what He is Himself by sending out His spirit upon them; just as the "tincture of gold"—that elixir of which alchemists dreamed—could transmute all other metals to itself. For another reference to the "tincture" see Herbert's poem, quoted on p. 79.

P. 41.—Ben Jonson wrote very few religious poems, but these are the product of genuine feeling, if but little originality.

P. 42.—"To Heaven." The second line is explained by the third. "Melancholy" was in Jonson's day the name of a disease that was prescribed for. We might paraphrase by saying, Must I, because I am grieved for sin, be told my liver is out of order? In the next couplet he refers to the fashion of affecting melancholy. Cf. Shakespeare's *King John*, iv. 1, 13—

> "I remember, when I was in France,
> Young gentlemen would be as sad as night,
> Only for wantonness";

and the speeches of the "melancholy Jacques" in *As You Like It*.

P. 45.—Drummond's religious poetry is, for the most part, picturesque rather than devotional; but the lines here printed have a true ring about them.

P. 47.—The Rev. Robert Herrick was vicar of Dean Prior, near Totnes, in Devonshire, from 1629 to 1647, when he was ejected by the Puritans, and became Robert Herrick, Esq. (under which title he published his *Hesperides* in 1648), till the Restoration, after which he returned to his living, holding it till his death twelve years later. An evidence, if evidence were needed, that his religious poems were not merely professional and to catch preferment, lies in the fact that he taught them to his parishioners.

P. 53.—The Rev. Giles Fletcher (1588-1673) was vicar of Alderton in Suffolk, where, according to Fuller, he was not valued according to his worth by his "clownish, low-parted

NOTES

parishioners." He and his brother Phineas were devoted admirers and imitators of Spenser.

P. 61.—George Herbert (1593-1632), who was younger brother to Lord Herbert of Cherbury, took a brilliant degree at Cambridge and became Public Orator. For some time he expected court preferment, but his patrons died, and he eventually took orders. His short life at Bemerton is described by Walton as that of a saint. His " Temple " was posthumously printed (1632).

Herbert's poems are, if not the high-water mark of English devotional verse, yet its most characteristic expression, being the work of a scholar and a gentleman as well as a divine. His sense of rhythm was faultless, and his style exquisite. Observe on the one hand the skill with which he develops such an elaborate ode as " The Collar," and on the other his fine use of the regular metres. His fault was a too great fondness for conceits, by which some of his best poems are marred. A few passages are introduced at the close of the selection from poems which for this or other reasons could not be printed entire.

No poet except Donne is in such need of a commentator. Edition follows upon edition, but with no effort to clear up for the general reader Herbert's obscurities. A few notes follow on the chief difficulties of the poems here included.

The " Church Porch " is so called as containing rules of common morality and good breeding.

P. 64.—" Mattens," line 4. To "make a match" is to make an agreement, come to terms, and the sense intended seems to be: As I see Thou art waiting for my sacrifice to-day, I must even pay it. The penultimate verse is difficult. Herbert has been saying how marvellous it is that the Creator should care for the homage of each single creature, as He clearly does from the pains He spends upon it; whereas it is man who ought to devote himself to the Creator. Instead, however, of doing so, man attends to God's world with as much care as if it was his own. In the last verse the poet decides that it is possible so to study the world as not to miss God. " This new light " is the light of the new day.

P. 65.—" Praise," line 4, " I will pray to Thee to prevent my love ceasing."

Line 19.—" I can give Thee a higher place in my affections "; then the poet, perhaps for rhyme's sake, adds the irrelevant, " I cannot, of course, give Thee a higher place in heaven."

Line 25.—"After all this talk of praise, my praise is a poor thing; if continued for ever, it would fall short of expressing Thy mercy."

P. 67.—"The Pearl." The reference given by Herbert is Matt. xiii. 45, 46; the thought being that for the gospel's sake he counts learning, honour, and pleasure well exchanged.

Line 2.—*The press.* I have a feeling that Herbert intends a quibble here between the printing-press and some other, such as a wine or olive press. I don't know what kind of press would be fed by a "head" (*i.e.* fount) and "pipes," but there may be some confusion. In Zechariah's vision the lamps are fed by "pipes" from the olive trees.

Line 5, 6.—Astrology, Natural Science, Alchemy.

Line 8.—*Stock and surplus* may be the learning we inherit, and that which we add to it.

Line 13.—I know how to gauge by the rules of courtesy, who wins in a contest of doing favours; when each party is urged by ambition to do all he can by look or deed to win the world and bind it on his back. In Whitney's emblems there is a picture of a man trying to swim with a bundle tied to his back, as in the familiar allegory of Bunyan.

Line 18.—Honour includes also bravery, whether in defence of friends or in the duel.

Line 26.—*Store,* a favourite word with Herbert for " plenty."

Line 34.—*Seeled,* blinded, like a falcon. Cf. "Come, seeling night," in *Macbeth,* iii. 2, 46. The terms of the exchange, and the nature of the things exchanged (learning, etc.), are well understood by the poet; yet it is not his wisdom, but God's guidance, that has prompted the surrender.

"The Pulley," line 16.—*Rest,* an unfortunate quibble.

"Man's Medley." The thought in this poem is clearer than the expression. Man has double joys and sorrows answering to his double nature, but the soul's joys are to be preferred as lasting into the world beyond.

"The Collar" is, of course, conscience, the sense of duty, which in certain moods seems to be only an irritating restraint, self-imposed for no sufficient reason.

"The Pilgrimage," line 24.—*Which some call the wold.* Why Herbert adds this is not clear: it can hardly be only for rhyme's sake. He probably had in his mind Salisbury Plain, which in some parts of England, such as Lincolnshire, would no doubt have been called a "wold." The play on angel, and the coin so called, is perhaps obvious.

Line 36.—*A chair*, as our more luxurious generation might say, *a couch*.

"The Flower," line 3.—*Demean*, for demeanour, or more probably for *demesne*, an estate. The flowers not only have their own property of sweetness, but the passing of winter makes them still more pleasant.

Line 20.—*Is*, *i.e.* is in itself, or unchangeably; it is what it is by God's immediate ordinance.

"The Elixir," line 15.—*For Thy sake* is the "tincture" which makes every action bright, the "clause" that makes drudgery divine.

"Employment," line 11.—Joys await us in heaven; but how great they shall be we determine here, for they are "according to our work."

Line 21.—*Chain*, the chain of the universe, exemplified above by the links husbandry, flowers, bees, honey. The next line seems to mean, I am a weed, sole and single, out of relation to flowers and bees; but it is very obscurely expressed. *Reed* is for reed-instrument, such as the oboe or clarionet.

"Church Music." The date of Herbert's residence at Bemerton was 1630-33, so that the reference in line 8 is probably to the growing discontent of the Puritan party. The last stanza means, It consoles me to know I shall die before the worst of the troubles; for as it is I shall be comforted with church music on my dying bed; if it were forbidden, my loss would be great, for it is the usher to the door of heaven.

"Praise," line 4.—"To do a person right" was a courteous phrase for praising; the idea being that whatever praise was given was no more than desert.

P. 85.—Quarles (1592-1644) was a Royalist and Churchman, cup-bearer to the Princess Elizabeth, and secretary to Archbishop Ussher. His verse was immensely popular in his day, but has since fallen into oblivion, from which very little of it is likely to recover. The poems here printed from the "Divine Emblems" are the best of that collection.

P. 86, line 8.—"To *vie* was to hazard, to put down a certain sum upon a hand of cards; to *revie* was to cover it with a larger sum, by which the challenged became the challenger, and was to be *revied* in his turn with a proportionate increase of stake. This continued till one of the party lost courage and gave up the whole; or obtained for a stipulated sum a discovery of his adversary's cards; when the best hand swept the table."—Gifford.

P. 88.—A *tasker* is a thresher.

P. 90.—The dial here described is plainly a pocket instrument, furnished with a compass by which to set the gnomon. Not having seen one of the sort, I am uncertain whether the epithet "silken" is to be taken literally or metaphorically.

P. 94.—The name of Campion was unknown to this generation, although famous in his own, until Mr. Bullen reprinted the verses from his Song-Books. His praise has been well expressed in the line that Peele addressed to him:—

> "Thou
> That richly cloth'st conceit with well-made words."

His thought is luminous and his verse transparent. He is not perhaps quite so happy in religious as in love poetry.

P. 97.—A. W.'s verses were contributed to Davison's *Poetical Rhapsody* (1602). For the discussion as to his identity, the reader is referred to Mr. Bullen's preface to his edition of the *Rhapsody* (Bell, 1870). It would be a pity to see in his initials, as some suggest, but another form of the too familiar *anonymous writer*; but the mystery has not otherwise been solved.

P. 101.—This popular poem, founded on Damian's "Ad perennis vitae fontem" was first printed at the end of an anonymous poem, "The Song of Mary the Mother of Christ," 1601, and there initialed F. B. P. The text here followed is that of Mr. W. T. Brooke, of the British Museum (from a MS. there), who added an interesting selection of inedited poems to an edition of G. Fletcher's *Christ's Victory and Triumph* (Griffith & Farran). I have omitted six verses and grouped the remainder in sections.

P. 105.—Printed in Mr. Brooke's collection, referred to above (p. 206). It would seem to be founded upon Herbert's poem called "Decay."

P. 106.—From John Danyel's *Songs for the Lute, Viol, and Voice*.

P. 107.—"Let not the sluggish sleep," from William Byrd's *Psalms, Songs, and Sonnets*, 1611. "Yet if his majesty," from Christ Church MS., K. iii. 43-45. These three poems are borrowed from Mr. Bullen's *Lyrics from Elizabethan Song-Books;* for the last especially every reader will be grateful to him.

P. 109.—Crashaw (1613-49) was ejected from his fellowship at Peterhouse by the Parliament in 1644, and retired to Paris, where he joined the Roman Church. For several years he was in distress, till by Cowley's introduction to Queen Henrietta Maria he obtained a post in the household of Cardinal Palotta, and afterwards was made sub-canon of Loretto. His English poems were printed in 1646 under the title of *Steps to the Temple: Sacred Poems, with other Delights of the Muses*. Crashaw is so fine a poet that it is a pity he took so sentimental a view of religion. If Herbert with his restrained passion represents the spirit of the Anglican communion, Crashaw with his fervour and want of taste may well stand for the Roman. The passages here chosen, while they exhibit his genius, as it has never before been exhibited [in an anthology, are as free as possible from the worst defects of his manner.

P. 126.—William Habington (1605-1654) wrote a series of poems upon his wife under the style of Castara. His religious poetry is almost entirely upon the grave. The example here given is much above the average of his writing.

P. 128.—From *Religio Medici* (ii. 117, ed. Pickering): "In fine, so like death [is sleep], I dare not trust it without my prayers, and an half adieu unto the world, and take my farewell in a colloquy with God. [Here follows the poem.] This is the dormitive I take to bed-ward; I need no other laudanum than this to make me sleep: after which I close mine eyes in security, content to take my leave of the sun, and sleep unto the resurrection."

P. 129.—"Morning Hymn" is from "Paradise Lost," v. 153. "The Spacious Firmament" is from viii. 100. With the former may be compared Thomson's "Hymn" on the Seasons, and Coleridge's "Hymn before Sunrise in the Vale of Chamouni," both much inferior compositions. "God's Providence" is from "Samson Agonistes," 652-704; 293-299; 2745-48.

P. 137.—Jeremy Taylor (1613-67), the most eloquent of English divines, told his friend John Evelyn that in writing verse he had only the use of his left hand, and it is astonishing to see how small skill he had in that art. His odes are but collections of lines of various lengths, with no unity and little mutual relation.

P. 141.—The Rev. Alexander Rosse was one of Charles I.'s chaplains. The few verses here given are from a poem in *Mel*

Heliconium, or Poetical Honey Gathered out of the Weeds of Parnassus (1646); quoted by Mr. Abbey in *Religious Thought in Old English Verse.*

P. 142.—The Rev. John Mason (1646–94), rector of Water Stratford, Bucks., was distinguished in his day for millenarian notions. Latterly his mind became unhinged; he ceased to use the Church prayers, and announced that the reign of the saints was about to begin. The succeeding rector had to exhume his body to convince the parishioners that he had really died. His *Songs of Praise* were published in 1683.

P. 147.—Dr. Joseph Beaumont (1616–99), Master of Jesus College, Cambridge, and afterwards of Peterhouse, was the author of a religious poem called "Psyche" in the Spenserian stanza of some 30,000 lines, as well as of minor poems. These have been collected and edited by Dr. Grosart.

P. 148.— Henry More (1614–87), one of the so-called Cambridge Platonists, wrote a philosophical poem also in the Spenserian stanza, called "A Platonick Song of the Soul," with parts called Psychozoia, Psychathanasia, Anti-psychopannychia, etc. The poems here given are from *Minor Poems,* 1647.

P. 151.—Richard Baxter (1615–91), the celebrated Presbyterian divine, author of the *Saints' Everlasting Rest,* was a lengthy writer. "The Exit" has thirty-one verses, of which twelve are here printed. The full title of his *Poetical Fragments* is as follows:— "Heart Employment with God and Itself. The concordant discord of a broken-healed heart, sorrowing-rejoicing, fearing-hoping, dying-living. Written partly for himself, and partly for near friends in sickness and other deep affliction" (1699). To which the next year were added others, "written for himself, and communicated to such as are more for serious verse than smooth."

P. 156.—Andrew Marvell (1621–78) is one of the few English poets whose style can be called exquisite. Lamb speaks of his "witty delicacy." The period of his poetical production, other than satires, was the two years (1650–52) he spent at Nun Appleton as tutor to the daughter of Lord Fairfax. By him he was introduced to Milton, and became assistant Latin secretary, and subsequently M.P. for Hull. He was a Royalist, who is remembered as the panegyrist of Cromwell, and the refuser of a bribe from Charles II. At the Restoration he was able to protect Milton.

P. 162.—Henry Vaughan (1621-75), called the Silurist, as an inhabitant of South Wales, owed to Herbert both his conversion and much of his inspiration as a poet. What the debt exactly was the present writer has endeavoured to estimate in a preface to the edition of Vaughan in the "Muses' Library" (Laurence & Bullen). But Vaughan's mysticism, the predominating quality of his best verse, gives him independent rank. At his best he can soar far beyond Herbert's range, but he lacks Herbert's fine sense of style, and rarely maintains a high level throughout a long poem. The pieces here given present him at his best and most equable.

P. 164.—"The Retreat" is interesting, besides its own merits, as the germ of Wordsworth's great ode on the "Intimations of Immortality." We know that a copy of the rare *Silex Scintillans* was in Wordsworth's library.

P. 165.—The title of this poem seems to be Vaughan's own version of Romans viii. 19, the words *exerto capite*, "with head outstretched," having no parallel in the Vulgate version or Beza's.

P. 171.—Campbell borrowed from this poem in his "Rainbow" the lines—

"How came *the world's gray fathers* forth
    To watch thy sacred sign."

P. 178.—From *The Pilgrim's Progress*, Part II. This sweet little song has no less sweet a setting. "Now as they were going along and talking, they espied a Boy feeding his Father's Sheep. The Boy was in very mean Cloaths, but of a very fresh and well-favoured Countenance, and as he sate by himself he sung. Hark, said *Mr. Greatheart*, to what the Shepherd's Boy saith. So they hearkened, and he said—

'He that is down needs fear no fall,'" etc.

P. 179.—The Rev. John Norris was rector of Bemerton, Herbert's parish, for twenty years (1691-1711); it was, however, before going there that he published his *Poems* (1684), which are far removed from Herbert's inspiration, though they occasionally suggest his manner. The thought is usually virile, but the attitudinising expression often rises no higher than Christopher Harvey's lucubrations in "The Synagogue," which are bound up with too many copies of "The Temple."

There is great dignity in one piece on "The Passion of the Virgin Mother," which opens—

"Nigh to the fatal and yet sovereign wood."

P. 180.—The "Christmas Poems" and the "Litany" are from *The Moravian Hymn-Book;* a collection made in 1754, and including many well-known seventeenth-century poems, some curiously trimmed into shape for singing.

P. 182.—The "Ways of Wisdom" I borrow from Mr. W. T. Brooke's edition of Giles Fletcher already referred to, who found it in a manual of devotions.

P. 184.—"The Child's Death" is my second debt to Mr. Abbey; he quotes it as an anonymous poem of the seventeenth century, from Emily Taylor's *Flowers and Fruits from Old English Gardens.* It has a remarkably modern air about it.

P. 185.—Dr. Isaac Watts (1674-1748), the celebrated Nonconformist divine, suffered all his life from infirm health, so that there is no reason to doubt the sincerity of these certainly beautiful verses. This and another on a kindred subject, called "Happy Frailty," are much the best of his *Lyric Poems,* which are to our modern taste intolerable for the most part. His fame, however, rests securely on his hymns, the best of which, "O God, our help in ages past," and "Jesus shall reign where'er the sun," are among the best in the language.

P. 187.—John Byrom (1691-1763), famous in his day as the inventor of a system of shorthand, is now remembered as the friend of William Law, whose periods it delighted him to turn into doggerel verse, and still better as the author of several epigrams, notably those on the King and Pretender, and Handel and Buononcini. His poems were published in 1773, and his very interesting diary was edited for the Chetham Society in 1854. The well-known hymn, "Christians, awake," is shortened from a poem of his.

P. 191.—Charles Wesley (1707-68) wrote in his lifetime over 6000 hymns for the Methodist Society, to form "a body of experimental and practical divinity." Among these "Jesu, lover of my soul," is by far the best, and in its own kind may claim to be the best hymn in the language. Others almost equally popular are his Christmas hymn, "Hark, how all the welkin rings," and "Come, let us join our friends above," which, however, usually appear in modern hymnals as "Hark, the herald angels sing," and "Let saints on earth in concert sing."

The poem on "Wrestling Jacob," here given, was said by Watts to be "worth all the verses which he himself had ever written."

P. 194.—William Cowper (1731-1800) became a poet at the suggestion of his friends, to relieve a melancholic mind from feeding upon itself. At the suggestion of the Rev. John Newton, the curate of Olney in Buckinghamshire, he co-operated with him in writing hymns for the church there. The sweetest of Cowper's, "Hark, my soul," is too well known to quote; but two others of the collection, which are rather poems than hymns, are here given. For the rest, his verse, though often serious, offers no material for a *Lyra Sacra*.

P. 196.—Thomas Chatterton (1752-70) came of a long line of sextons at St. Mary Redcliffe, Bristol, and, having access to the muniment room, fell in love with antiquity. His first poems were pseudo-antiques, the so-called Rowley poems, which imposed on Horace Walpole. When he was eighteen, his indentures with an attorney were cancelled for some supposed irreverence, and he went to try his fortune in London. For four months he battled with the publishers and the public, and then took arsenic. Among his best pieces are some of the songs in *Aella*. Except for the second line of the third stanza, the poem here given is remarkably inartificial; two stanzas are omitted before the last.

P. 198.—The Rev. George Crabbe (1754-1832), the son of a salt-master at Aldeburgh, who at twenty-six went up to London to seek his fortune in literature, fared no less hardly there than Chatterton, but was older and had less of the pride of genius. After repulses in high quarters where he had solicited patronage, he appealed to Burke, who befriended him, and henceforth his life was a smooth one. He was a close observer of the Suffolk peasantry, and his "Tales from the Hall" are life-like studies of great power and pathos. The poem here given is from "Sir Eustace Grey." It is supposed to be a Methodist hymn, remembered in a madhouse, and Crabbe half-apologises for it in a note: "The verses are not intended to make any religious persuasion appear ridiculous; though evidently enthusiastic in language, they are not meant to convey any impropriety of sentiment." Would that Crabbe had more often allowed himself in such enthusiasm! The lines appear to be modelled on a poem of Herbert's, "Come, my Way, my Truth, my Life."

P. 199.—William Blake (1757-1827) offers less material to the religious anthologist than might be anticipated from the writer of so many prophetical books, owing partly to the cryptic style he too often employed, and partly to a few eccentricities of thought, which he again and again repeats, to the disfigurement of many fine poems. To those given in the text should perhaps have been added the following from the Songs of Innocence, "On Another's Sorrow," which, though almost infantile in expression, is none the less lovely:

> "Can I see another's woe
> And not be in sorrow too?
> Can I see another's grief,
> And not seek for kind relief?
>
> Can I see a falling tear
> And not feel my sorrow's share?
> Can a father see his child
> Weep, nor be with sorrow filled?
>
> Can a mother sit and hear
> An infant groan, an infant fear?
> No, no; never can it be—
> Never, never can it be.
>
> And can He, who smiles on all,
> Hear the wren, with sorrows small—
> Hear the small bird's grief and care,
> Hear the woes that infants bear,
>
> And not sit beside the nest,
> Pouring pity in their breast?
> And not sit the cradle near,
> Weeping tear on infant's tear?
>
> And not sit both night and day,
> Wiping all our tears away?
> Oh no! never can it be!
> Never, never can it be!
>
> He doth give His joy to all;
> He becomes an infant small;
> He becomes a man of woe;
> He doth feel the sorrow too.

> Think not thou canst sigh a sigh,
> And thy Maker is not by;
> Think not thou canst weep a tear,
> And thy Maker is not near.
>
> Oh, He gives to us His joy,
> That our grief He may destroy;
> Till our grief is fled and gone,
> He doth sit by us and moan."

P. 203.—It has seemed better to select from Wordsworth the earlier and more general religious poems, which are certainly poetical, rather than the later and more dogmatic, such as "The Primrose of the Rock," "Inscriptions in a Hermit's Cell," or some of the Ecclesiastical Sonnets. From the great Ode it seemed allowable to extract the two parts which form its pith. The editor may be pardoned for pointing out to his younger readers that the opening lines on page 211 are to be paraphrased: "O joy, that there is still some life in our embers, namely, the *remembrance* of the departed glory." In explanation of the passage that follows, Wordsworth himself may be heard: "Nothing was more difficult for me in childhood than to admit the notion of death as a state applicable to my own being. It was not so much from feelings of animal vivacity that my difficulty came, as from a sense of the indomitableness of the spirit within me. I used to brood over the stories of Enoch and Elijah, and almost to persuade myself that, whatever might become of others, I should be translated in something of the same way to heaven. With a feeling congenial to this, I was often unable to think of external things as having external existences, and I communed with all that I saw as something not apart from, but inherent in, my own immaterial nature. Many times while going to school have I grasped at a wall or tree to recall myself from this abyss of idealism to the reality. At that time I was afraid of such processes. In later periods of life I have deplored, as we have all reason to do, a subjugation of an opposite character, and have rejoiced over the remembrances, as is expressed in the lines—

> 'Obstinate questionings,' etc."

It will be understood that the two *buts* in the lines "But for those obstinate questionings" and "But for those first affections" are co-ordinate, both depending on the "Not for these I raise" which, considering the line above, "for that which is *most worthy to be blest*," we may be bold to construe "Not *only* for these I raise."

P. 213.—It is no less true of Coleridge than of Wordsworth, that he is commonly most religious when he makes least effort to be so, besides being far more poetical. Accordingly, the editor has preferred the poem "To his Child," extracted from "Frost at Midnight," and the fragment taken from the "Ode to Joy," before the "Religious Musings" and the "Ode in the Vale of Chamouni."

P. 218.—Hartley Coleridge (1796–1849) eldest son of Samuel Taylor Coleridge, who with his father's weakness of will inherited also some of his genius, lived most of his life in the Lake Country. Wordsworth's ode to him, at six years old, besides being a singularly beautiful poem, showed great insight into his character. His most successful poetical performances are the sonnets, which he wrote at a jet without labour or polishing.

P. 220.—No better criticism of Keble's *Christian Year* was ever penned than that of Dr. MacDonald in *England's Antiphon*: "Excellent, both in regard of their literary and religious merits, true in feeling and thorough in finish, the poems always remind me of Berlin work in iron—hard and delicate." As the book is well known to all readers of religious verses, the editor has felt more at liberty to print a collection of "beauties" which might escape notice, rather than complete poems. The unrhymed ode at the end seems to reach Keble's high-water mark.

P. 231.—Mrs. Hemans, *née* Browne (1793–1835), is remembered now chiefly by one or two lyrics such as "The Better Land," and "The Homes of England," which have been set to music. She was a very fluent writer, and wrote with genuine feeling, but her style and sentiment are now old-fashioned.

P. 232.—From Cardinal Newman's literary executor, Father Neville, of the Birmingham Oratory, I have received permission to print three of the poems from *Verses on Various Occasions*.

P. 236.—The Rev. John Sterling (1806–43) was a brilliant Cambridge man who for a time became curate to Julius Hare at Hurstmonceaux. He will owe what fame he retains to Carlyle's life of him.

P. 237.—For leave to include so large a selection from Archbishop Trench's poems, I am indebted to the generosity of his son, Mr. A. Chenevix Trench.

NOTES

P. 251.—Faber (1814–63), son of the vicar of Calverley, Yorks., and himself for three years Rector of Elton, Huntingdonshire, followed Newman to Rome in 1845. He founded the branch of Oratorians in London, now settled at Brompton. His hymns are among the most popular in current collections.

P. 261.—The name of T. T. Lynch is well-known in Nonconformist circles as that of a hymn-writer, but he well deserves wider recognition. The poems here given are from *The Rivulet*, a book of verses first published in 1855, and several times augmented.

P. 267.—These songs of Charles Kingsley's are from *The Saints' Tragedy* (1848).

P. 266-274.—For permission to print these poems I am much indebted to Mrs. A. H. Clough and Mrs. Matthew Arnold respectively.

P. 275.—This poem was first printed in the 2nd edition of Fosbery's *Poems for the Sick and Suffering* (Rivington, 1850). Mr. Blackburne (1821–59) was educated at Queen's College, Oxford, and after some time spent in literary work on the *Athenæum*, he took orders. Two of his letters are printed in Hartley Coleridge's Memoirs.

P. 277.—Mr. Coventry Patmore has courteously allowed me to choose five poems from *The Unknown Eros* (1877).

P. 285.—Shortened, with the author's leave, from a poem in *Organ Songs*.

P. 287.—The poems of Dora Greenwell have not of late met with the appreciation they deserve. A large part of Messrs. Bell & Daldy's edition of *Carmina Crucis* was sold off as a remainder, and may still be bought of the purchaser, Mr. Gibbings of Bury Street, Bloomsbury. I have to thank Miss Greenwell's biographer, the Rev. W. Dorling, for obtaining the leave of her brother and literary executor to this selection.

P. 295.—The first three poems by Miss Rossetti are from the "Goblin Market" volume, the third, "From House to Home," being an extract from a much longer piece so called. For leave to include them my thanks are due to author and publishers (Messrs. MacMillan) conjointly. The rest of the selection is from the volume entitled *Verses*, by leave of the Society for Promoting Christian Knowledge.

P. 304.—From "St. Paul" : the text is printed by the author's desire from the latest edition (1894).

P. 311.—From *Poems* (1876).

P. 313.—A selection of poems by the late Father Hopkins, S.J. appeared, with a critical notice by Mr. Robert Bridges, in Miles's *Poets of the Century*, vol. viii. Those in this anthology, which are all now printed for the first time, are given by kind leave of the poet's father, Mr. Manley Hopkins. Several manuscript versions exist, but the text here printed has the author's final corrections. The editor has preferred to fill the space at his disposal with uupublished pieces, but the reader who finds these to his taste should turn to those in Mr. Miles's volume, which are also religious for the most part. One fragment of a hymn may be given as a specimen—

> "Thee, God, I came from, to thee go,
> All day long I like fountain flow
> From thy hand out, swayed about
> Mote-like in thy mighty glow.
>
> What I know of thee I bless,
> As acknowledging thy stress
> On my being, and as seeing
> Something of thy holiness.
>
> Once I turned from thee and hid,
> Bound on what thou hadst forbid;
> Sow the wind I would; I sinned:
> I repent of what I did.
>
> Bad I am, but yet thy child.
> Father, be thou reconciled.
> Spare thou me, since I see
> With thy might that thou art mild.
>
> I have life left with me still,
> And thy purpose to fulfil;
> Yes, a debt to pay thee yet:
> Help me, sir, and so I will."

P. 317.—Mr. Bridges' sonnets are from *The Growth of Love*, privately printed by the Rev. H. Daniel (1889); the other pieces from *Shorter Poems* (4th ed., 1894).

P. 327.—Digby Mackworth-Dolben (1848–67) was drowned while bathing. His verses, a few of which are here printed for the first time, show remarkable poetical gifts. "The Shrine" is an original and most successful contribution to a

NOTES

class of poems where success is rare and difficult, poems of filial love; and should be widely popular. Another poem, somewhat more youthful in manner, and bearing plain traces of Rossetti's influence, may be printed here for the beauty of many of its lines. The first verse is an especially fine piece of imagination—

"Sing me the men ere this
Who, to the gate that is
A cloven pearl, uprapt,
The big white bars between
With dying eyes have seen
The sea of jasper, lapt
About with crystal sheen.

And all the far pleasance
Where linkèd angels dance,
With scarlet wings that fall
Magnifical, or spread
Most sweetly overhead,
In fashion musical
Of cadenced lutes instead.

Sing me the town they saw,
Withouten fleck or flaw;
Aflame, more fine than glass
Of fair Abbayes the boast,—
More glad than wax of cost
Doth make at Candlemas
The Lifting of the Host.

Where many Knights and Dames,
With new and wondrous names,
One great Laudate psalm
Go singing down the street.
'Tis peace upon their feet,
In hand 'tis pilgrim palm
Of Holy Land so sweet.

Where Mother Mary walks
'Mid silver lily stalks,
Star-tirèd, moon-bedight:
Where Cecily is seen,
With Dorothy in green,
And Magdalen all white,
The maidens of the Queen.

> Sing on—the steps untrod,
> The temple that is God—
> Where incense doth ascend,
> Where mount the cries and tears
> Of all the dolorous years,
> With moan that ladies send
> Of durance and sore fears.
>
> And Him who sitteth there,
> The Christ of purple hair,
> And great eyes, deep with ruth,
> Who is, of all things fair,
> That shall be, or that were,
> The sum and very Truth.
> Then add a little prayer,
>
> That since all these be so,
> Our Liege, who doth us know,
> Would 'fend from Sathanas,
> And bring us, of His grace
> To that His joyous place,
> So we the doom may pass
> And see Him in the Face."

P. 327.—From *Underwoods* (1887).
P. 330.—From *Poems* (1893).

INDEX

	PAGE
A chill blank world. Yet over the utmost sea	302
A genial moment oft has given	239
Ah, God, alas	279
Ah, that sharp thrill through all my frame	311
Ah, what time wilt thou come? when shall that cry	176
Ah yes; we tell the good and evil trees	283
All day among the cornfields of the plain	292
All glory else besides ends with our breath	24
A naked house, a naked moor	328
And art Thou come, blest Babe, and come to me	180
And art Thou come with us to dwell	293
And did those feet in ancient times	199
And do they so? have they a sense	165
And for the heaven's wide circuit, let it speak	131
And is there care in heaven? And is there love	14
As body when the soul has fled	45
As due by many titles I resign	32
As earth's pageant passes by	147
As perchance carvers do not faces make	40
A tear is an intellectual thing	202
At the round earth's imagin'd corners blow	33
Author of life, revive my dying sprite	95
Awake, thou wintry earth	275
Ay me, poor soul, whom bound in sinful chains	97
Be not afraid to pray, to pray is right	219
Blest pair of sirens, pledges of heaven's joy	136

	PAGE
But now the second morning from her bow'r	58
Can I not sin, but thou wilt be	49
Cheer up, desponding soul	188
Christ, for whose only love I keep me clean	324
Christ when He died	110
Collect thy soul into one sphere	148
Come, O Thou Traveller unknown	191
Comrades, haste! the tents' tall shading	224
Courage, my soul! now learn to wield	156
Dear babe, that sleepest cradled by my side	214
Death, be not proud, though some have called thee	34
Deep in the warm vale the village is sleeping	268
Die to thy root, sweet flower	290
Do not their souls, who 'neath the altar wait	232
Draw near as early as we may	226
England, awake! awake! awake!	199
Eternal Father, who didst all create	322
Eternal Mover, whose diffusèd glory	29
Eternal Truth, almighty, infinite	20
Even such is Time, that takes in trust	12
False world, thou liest: thou canst not lend	85
Far among the lonely hills	267
Father of heav'n, and Him by whom	35
Fever and fret and aimless stir	253
Fly, envious Time, till thou run out thy race	137
Frail Life! in which, through mists of human breath	125
Frail multitude! whose giddy law is list	55
Frail soul, how long shall veils thy graces shroud	22
Gaze but upon the house where man embow'rs	59
Give me my scallop-shell of quiet	12
God moves in a mysterious way	194
God's child in Christ adopted, Christ my all	215
God when He takes my goods and chattels hence	52
God, who at sundry times, in manners many	304

	PAGE
God, who with thunders and great voices kept	247
Good and great God, can I not think of Thee	42
Had I a glance of Thee, my God	187
Happy those early days when I	164
Hark how the birds do sing	70
Hath not the potter power to make his clay	190
Hear me, O God	41
Heaven in the depth and height is seen	221
He did but float a little way	184
Hence is't that I am carried towards the west	37
Here in this little bay	277
He that is down needs fear no fall	178
Hierusalem, my happy home	101
Honey in the lion's mouth	242
How fresh, O Lord, how sweet and clean	77
How happy is he born and taught	28
How know I that it looms lovely	299
How long, great God, how long must I	179
How shall I sing that Majesty	142
How should I praise Thee, Lord! how should my rhymes	84
How welcome, in the sweet still hour	228
Humble we must be, if to heaven we go	52
I asked for peace	326
I cannot ope mine eyes	64
If as a flower doth spread and die	80
If I could shut the gate against my thoughts	106
If I have faltered more or less	327
I fled Him, down the nights and down the days	330
I give myself to prayer	264
I have deserved a thick Egyptian damp	166
I have desired to go	315
I heard an angel singing	200
I heard the wild beasts in the woods complain	256
I know the ways of learning; both the head	67
In a valley of this restless mind	6
In spring the green leaves shoot	287
In the hour of my distress	47
I said, This task is keen	287

	PAGE
I say to thee, do thou repeat	237
I sing the Name which none can say	111
Is this a fast to keep	50
I struck the board, and cried, No more	72
It is a beauteous evening, calm and free	208
I travell'd on, seeing the hill where lay	74
I was angry with my friend	202
I will accept thy will to do and be	296
Jesu, Lord, that madest me	4
Jesus that sprang of Jesse's root	1
Joy, sweetest life-born joy, where dost thou dwell	317
King of Glory, King of Peace	65
Lamb of God, my Saviour	181
Leave me, O love which reachest but to dust	19
Let not the sluggish sleep	106
Let praise devote thy work, and skill employ	322
Let thy repentance be without delay	190
Life out of death, light out of darkness springs	45
Like to the arctic needle, that doth guide	90
Lord, all things everywhere	261
Lord, bind me up and let me lie	168
Lord, come away	139
Lord, many times I am aweary quite	239
Lord, what is man? why should he cost you	116
Lord, what unvalued treasures crowned	105
Lord, when the sense of Thy sweet grace	109
Lord, with what care hast Thou begirt us round	66
Love God, and love your neighbour. Watch and pray	84
Love, thou art absolute, sole lord	119
Many are the sayings of the wise	133
Mark how, a thousand streams in one	223
Methinks we do as fretful children do	249
Most glorious Lord of Life, that on this day	15
Mutual forgiveness of each vice	202
My genial spirits fail	216
My God, permit me not to be	187

	PAGE
My heart leaps up when I behold	208
My hovering thoughts would fly to heaven	21
My little son, who look'd from thoughtful eyes	281
My Lord, my Love was crucified	144
My soul, go boldly forth	153
My soul is like a bird, my flesh the cage	93
My spirit longeth for Thee	188
Never weather-beaten sail more willing bent to shore	96
New doth the sun appear	46
No faith towards God can e'er subsist with wrath	190
Not in the evening's eyes	118
Not in the lucid intervals of life	206
Not Thou from us, O Lord, but we	238
Not to know vice at all, and keep true state	43
Now of Thy love we deem	222
O all wide places, far from feverous towns	285
O England, full of sin, but most of sloth	61
O Father, in that hour	231
O foolish soul, to make thy count	303
Oft have I sat in secret sighs	186
O God, whose thunder shakes the sky	196
O grace, where is the joy	23
O happy arms where cradled lies	220
O huge and most unspeakable impression	15
O ignorant poor man, what dost thou bear	26
Old things need not be therefore true	269
O Lord, fulfil Thy will	299
O sacred Providence, who from end to end	82
O soul of Jesus, sick to death	254
O that some soul o'erweighed	292
O Thou great Power, in whom I move	31
O thou undaunted daughter of desires	124
Our birth is but a sleep and a forgetting	210
O were I ever what I am sometimes	266
O years, and age, farewell	48
O youngë freshë folkës, he or she	11
Passing away, saith the World, passing away	295

	PAGE
Pilgrim, burden'd with thy sin	198
Poor soul, the centre of my sinful earth	100
Rise, heir of fresh eternity	109
Sacred and secret hand	170
Sacred Religion, mother of form and fear	24
Said a sick and lonely child	288
Say not, the struggle nought availeth	269
See, how the orient dew	159
See, through the heavenly arch	263
She gave with joy her virgin breast	213
Since Christ embraced the cross itself, dare I	39
Since I am coming to that holy room	37
Since in a land not barren still	167
Since succour to the feeblest of the wise	277
Since to be loved endures	319
Sing aloud, His praise rehearse	150
Sin is with man at morning break	225
Sleep, sleep, old sun! thou canst not have repast	39
Sooner or later, yet at last	300
So spake the hoary thyme	289
Stern daughter of the voice of God	203
Still young and fine! but what is still in view	171
Stones towards the earth descend	189
Surely if each one saw another's heart	84
Sweetest of sweets, I thank you: when displeasure	81
Sweetest Saviour, if my soul	81
Sweet voices! seldom mortal ear	240
Tax not the royal saint with vain expense	209
Teach me, my God and King	79
The bird that sees a dainty bower	83
The dappled die-away	316
The deep knell dying down, the mourners pause	229
The door of death is made of gold	202
The just shall live by faith, and why? that faith	218
The Lord will happiness divine	195
The man of life upright	94
The merry world did on a day	71

	PAGE
Then earth and heaven were rolled up like a scroll	297
The pilot's skill how can we know	141
There is an awful quiet in the air	218
There is a shrine whose golden gate	323
These are Thy glorious works, Parent of good	129
These beauteous forms	205
These meagre rhymes which a returning mood	321
These sweeter far than lilies are	182
The spacious firmament on high	185
The world can neither give nor take	145
The world is charged with the grandeur of God	314
The world's a floor, whose swelling heaps retain	87
The world,—what a world, ah me	303
They are all gone into the world of light	174
They are at rest	234
Think, and be careful what thou art within	190
Think ye the spires that glow so bright	228
This world is unto God a work of art	320
Thou art not Truth, for he that tries	169
Thou bid'st me come away	51
Though heaven's above and earth's below	251
Though late, my heart, yet turn at last	98
Thou hast given me a heart to desire	291
Thou hast made me, and shall Thy work decay	32
Thou who dost dwell alone	271
Thou who on sin's wages starvest	313
Thou whose nature cannot sleep	128
Thou who taught'st the blind man's sight	140
Through that pure virgin shrine	172
Throw away Thy rod	75
Thus it shall be a lifetime, ne'er to meet	312
'Tis but a foil at best, and that's the most	89
To halls of heavenly truth admission wouldst thou win	245
To see a world in a grain of sand	201
Truth fails not ; but her outward forms that bear	209
We cannot kindle when we will	273
Weep not for me	233
Weighing the stedfastness and state	162
Weigh me the fire ; or canst thou find	51

	PAGE
We scatter seeds with careless hand	227
We seek to know the moving of each sphere	27
What are we set on earth for? Say, to toil	247
What hath man done that man shall not undo	53
What if this present were the world's last night	40
When first thy eyes unveil, give thy soul leave	162
When God at first made man	69
When I consider how my light is spent	135
When I see childhood on the threshold seize	320
When I survey the bright	126
When prayer delights thee least, then learn to say	243
When some belovèds, 'neath whose eyelids lay	248
When some belovèd voice that was to you	249
When up to nightly skies we gaze	236
Where lies the land to which the ship would go	270
Why should we faint and fear to live alone	227
Wilt thou forgive that sin where I begun	36
Ye flaming Powers, and wingèd warriors bright	132
Yet if his majesty our sovereign lord	107

www.ingramcontent.com/pod-product-compliance
Lightning Source LLC
Chambersburg PA
CBHW030400230426
43664CB00007BB/678